To: Pam & [...]

From: Leon Wheel #37

Prov 3:5-6

Beyond the Locker Room

This book is an original production of Random Adventures
Publishing, Charlotte, NC.

Cover design by Diana Wade. Text design by Diana Wade.

ISBN: 978-0-9909865-2-2

# Beyond the Locker Room

*Developing Your Game Plan for Life's Transitions*

Your Journey, Your Path

Leonard T. Wheeler

To my daughter, Lindsey,
as she enters her first big transition

# Contents

# Acknowledgments

There are hundreds of men and women who have contributed to my life over the years. This book can't contain all the gratitude I feel for their contributions, but please know that I'm extremely humbled and grateful. The type of transition and growth that we are advocating is never a solo endeavor.

I want to thank Corey May for being the first person to assist me in putting my vision on paper. I appreciate you, "Mizz," and then pass the baton to Leslie Satchell, who has been a loyal friend for years. Thanks, "Les." Then here comes Betsy Thorpe, who has also been a blessing to me during this project. Thanks so much, "Bets."

Thanks to my book graphic designer, Diana Wade, and my copyeditor, Maya Packard, for having patience during the writing of this book.

Thanks to Lincoln Financial and Lee Small and Pete Mastrotouno for hanging in there with me and believing that the book would be completed. Thanks to my game on Nation family, Blair Bloomston and Steve Shenbaum, for writing about Coins.

Thanks to my childhood brother and friend Dale Davis for always being supportive of my crazy endeavors. Thanks to Troy Vincent, Hardy Nickerson, Eugene Robinson, Charlotte Smith, Tracy Perlman, Dr. Will Mayer, and Andre Collins, for answering the call during the writing of this book and sharing your stories.

Thanks to my high school coach Rodney Walker and mentors David Gandy, David Hair, and Reggie Rice for the sound advice and sometimes-tough accountability. I have so many friends and family to thank; it's just impossible to list them all. But I would be remiss not to say thank you to the late Dr. Myles Munroe, who had committed to writing a chapter on Purpose in this book.

I sincerely want to thank my entire family for the commitment, prayers and guidance you have offered me over the years. I wouldn't be the person I am or be where I am today without your continuous love and support.

To all of you who continue to encourage, inspire, and assist as I GROW: Thank you!

And finally, thanks to my Lord and Savior Jesus Christ for providing me with an awesome team and giving me the strength and fortitude to finish my first book.

## About This Book

You're walking off the field or the court, and you look back one more time while asking the question: *Is this it?* You walk out of the locker room after the last game of your high school, college, or professional career with all your gear in your hand and you ask the question: *Now what?*

We have all heard over and over that transition is difficult, but the reality of it doesn't truly set in until it's happening to you personally.

All types of sports analogies will be used throughout this book, but it was my goal to make the information here applicable to anyone going through any type of transition. Whether you are switching jobs, leaving a sport, or going back to work after being at home with your kids, this book will assist you in being able to take the correct steps and open your mind to endless possibilities. I believe that every parent of an athlete, and athletes themselves, should be required to read this book, because it will help you establish a game plan for life.

It is my belief that only you can honestly say where you are on your transition journey. If you don't have any idea as to where you are, welcome to the journey. This book will help to serve as a guide before, during, and after your transition.

We all are in different places, but there is one constant: we will all experience some emotional roller coasters during the transition process. In these pages, you will find some very helpful tips and hear some awesome testimonials from others who have made a successful transition—and some who didn't.

God gave me the vision for this book as a resource tool to use as an outline for my own transition. I both failed and succeeded in my transition, and had to learn that I wasn't alone. I surrounded myself with individuals who were wiser, smarter, and had more life experience than I, and I allowed them to help me. I had to learn to develop different levels of courage in order to take certain risks as I searched for my purpose after sports. Simon Sinek, in his book *Start With Why*, writes about how to be inspired to take the correct action while searching for your "Why." My hope for you is that by the end of reading this book, you will find your new purpose. I strive to make your transition journey smoother, and to encourage you to inspire others along on their journeys as well.

# Introduction:

## TRANSITIONS ARE INEVITABLE

Here is the story of a player I met recently on the road:

*I played nine years in the NFL and it's come to this:*

*Now, the highlight of my day—every single day since the start of football season—is showing up early to my daughter's school so that I can participate in recess with the kids. This is my reality. I am reduced to entertaining a class of five-year-olds, because every day is Tuesday and I don't know what else to do to pass the time. Oddly enough, I like interacting with the kids. The teacher told me that they are often so anxious about my arrival that she threatens to cancel my visits if they don't behave. I know it sounds crazy, but it's so nice to be needed.*

*I remember there was a time when several NFL teams were trying to sign me. Teams needed me. And, thinking introspectively, I realized that I needed them as much as they needed me. The NFL validated me in a way that nothing else had before. And football made me feel alive. My craft made me worthy—worthy of success, worthy of respect, and worthy of recognition to the point where I was so intoxicated by the experience, I was in a perpetual state of euphoria—until now.*

*I would compare today to a hangover, except for this one doesn't seem like it is ever going to go away. As I sit here at the start of week 8 watching* Monday Night Football *with my daughter, I crave being on that field. I miss the rush bad. How can I be an NFL player, but not play? And if I am not an NFL player, then who am I?*

*I tried to make a mental list of other things I could do, like what else can I do well, because I have to "win" at whatever I do next. This is what I came up with: OK, I can golf. Yeah, I am a beast on the green! I started to think about how much time I spent golfing, traveling to golf, hosting golf events, and shopping for golf weekends.*

*My mind wandered as I thought about all that football allowed me to experience. Man, I have been to some fabulous places, rubbed elbows with some powerful people, and was able to indulge in my free time to my heart's content. From model-like women, fine dining, and spa visits to high-end shopping, stuntin' at exclusive events, and sleep—believe me, I indulged every offseason.*

*But in this moment, none of it—and I mean none of it, seemed to translate into what's going to happen next as I wrestled with the thought of retiring.*

*So...I'll just call my agent tomorrow and put some fire under his ass because I'm really NOT ready to retire. I can still play, so I'll just keep playing.*

*My little internal reflection was cut short by my daughter tugging at my shirt to tell me that my cell phone was ringing. I jumped up to get it, thinking wouldn't this be divine intervention if it was my agent calling to tell me to head to the airport because a team wanted to see me work out. But, I wasn't so lucky. It was actually an old friend who used to be my marketing rep, calling for her quarterly check in.*

*Rep: Hey Jack, just calling to see what's up with you these days. How are you?*
*Me [lying]: I am awesome. Just trying to keep busy—you know, working out so I'll be ready when I get that call.*
*Rep: Oh, OK. I see—you think you'll get a call this late in the season?*
*Me [lying again]: Yeah. My agent said several teams have been calling and he's expecting one of them to pull the trigger soon and sign me.*
*Rep: Gotcha. I thought you had just decided to throw in the towel and retire?*
*Me: Nah, I can still play.*

*Rep: Don't torture yourself. You know it's OK to walk away. Nine years is a long time. You had a great run!*
*Me: Look, I need to go and get my daughter ready for bed. Can I call you back?*
*Rep: Sure, we'll catch up soon. Call me if you need me. Bye, Jack.*

*My rep always had a way of making me look in the mirror, even when I didn't want to. Dang, I am retired—and I didn't even know it.*
*What's next for me? I don't even know what to do now...*

*Beyond the Locker Room* was inspired when I first started to work with athletes such as this former player who were having problems transitioning into a new life once their athletic careers ended. As a former pro football player, I knew what they were going through—I had been there myself. What I soon came to realize was that the principles in helping someone transition from one career situation to the next are applicable to anyone who needs to make a shift and reorient their identity to encompass a new station in life.

Many athletes started out competing in sports as young children. Our fathers might have taken us to our first practice, or our moms, our coach, or maybe even a friend in our neighborhood. And we liked playing football, or baseball, basketball, lacrosse, soccer, or running track. For many of us, no matter what the sport, the goal was the same: to get as far as you can, and achieve as much as you can. The ultimate dream was to become a high school athlete, a college athlete, and then for some maybe a professional athlete—a rich and famous one.

Millions of kids dream about it, but only a few make it. We train, we practice with our teams, we eat right, we work with coaches, and we go to as many camps as possible to get better. We invest everything we have in attaining the fame and fortune we see our idols enjoy, until...well, frankly, we run out of gas. Then, eventually, we all become armchair participants—watching from the sidelines of the sport we loved and used to play.

So whether it's the locker room, the board room, the classroom, or any other figurative space that once defined you—prepare to move beyond that place. What I demonstrate in this book is that the skills learned on the field, on the court, and in the locker room can be transferred to the daily practices of anyone who wants to live a fulfilling, successful life. By transitioning your thoughts, your goals, and your skills, you can meet the next challenge that life has to offer with an effective game plan.

## Change is Certain, So Make Transformation Your Goal

Life is not without change: The people around you will change. Your circumstances will change. The world will change. Your needs and outlook on life will change as well. But the key to being victorious in life, despite many of these moving, often uncontrollable parts, is understanding that your transition to the next part of your life is a personal evolution and a huge opportunity to grow both internally and externally. *The Purpose Driven Life* by Rick Warren is a great resource.

LIVING A LIFE WITH PURPOSE, A LIFE WHERE YOUR GIFTS AND ASPIRATIONS TRULY MEET THE POTENTIAL WITHIN, MEANS TACKLING INEVITABLE TRANSITIONS AT EVERY STAGE OF YOUR LIFE.

Look back at your childhood aspirations: taking off the training wheels, moving up a grade in school, being assigned your first locker, reaching the age when you could play on a sports team, and even receiving your driver's license—did you ever see those points in your life as the absolute end of change? No. Chances are that you already knew how to think of your life as a series of transitions without even realizing it. You naturally knew when it was time for a new challenge or new stage. Sometimes it was based on age, but at other times you just knew you were ready for something else. Transition is more palatable when you understand it to be a process. It's a journey that will never end, and if you can start thinking like that today, your next inevitable transition will be simpler.

So ready or not, change is coming! However, it does not have to be intimidating. All that you have accomplished so far in life proves that you are more than capable of adjusting. Everyone's journey is different, but there is something to be said about seeing what may be ahead. Whether you can avoid it or prepare for it and plow through it, clarity about who you are and what you need and want in the process is pivotal. We have to remember that we are truly more than conquerors.

### Reflecting on the Locker Room

The locker room is a place that I knew and loved deeply as a high school, college, and professional football player. It's viewed as a safe haven for many athletes. The locker room is a place for camaraderie, joking around, and getting pumped up for the game. There's a lot of banter going on in there: guys cracking on each other and making light of the most sensitive insecurities, but it's all in fun—well, mostly. It's where you recover from a loss or celebrate a victory.

The locker room can be a comforting place—where teammates support each other and where coaches fire everyone up. Coaches admonish, motivate, encourage, chastise, and even father in the locker room, and players often hang on their every word. You understand that the locker room is where you get direction, a pat on the back, and sometimes, a bit of peace. And you become dependent on the feeling you get from the locker room and appreciate being a part of what feels like a family to you.

Coaches will sometimes affirm how athletes feel about the locker room by saying things like:

- "The only people who believe in us are in this locker room."
- "We're all we've got."
- "Look around: these are your brothers/sisters!"
- "Your teammates are counting on you."
- "Don't let the team down."
- "We have to trust each other."
- "Each one of you has a job to do."

As a football player, I was conditioned by that environment to live up to the expectations of the team and go above and beyond to perform for them, even on days when I wanted to give up. You fight for those in your locker room. You share ups and downs with them. You give and receive support. You become part of a unit that wants you and needs you—and it feels good and safe—to the point where being vulnerable is even acceptable. There's exposure from everywhere. Everyone, even the media in some cases, will see what's going on with you—your scars, your muscles, your injuries—and there are some who might even pick up on where you are mentally. Are you down, are you overconfident, and are you scared? Are you beating yourself up because you didn't execute well? No matter what state you are in, it all seems OK because it is the locker room. It is home. Who wouldn't want to stay there forever if they are getting what they need emotionally?

When I arrived to play with the Carolina Panthers in 1998, everything was still pretty new. The stadium looked fresh and modern, and so did the players' facilities. The team, founded in 1995, was young and still getting to know each other. I was so excited to be there and be a part of that time—never did it cross my mind that this would be the last locker room for me. I guess I was living in the moment, thinking I would stay there for a while.

But the locker room has a way of putting you out, even if you are not ready. For some, it's age. For others, it's declining skills. For me, it was an injury. In the blink of an eye, I blew out my ACL and meniscus running down the field on a routine kickoff in front of about 60,000 fans. As I was lying on the field, I remember thinking, "Oh my God. No! I just blew out my knee! Now what?" I went into the locker room with my team chaplain Mike Bunckley, and started crying in total fear of what was to come.

Suddenly, I was on the outside looking into the window of the game that I'd been playing since the age of five. After two years of rehab and retearing my meniscus, I wanted to go back and play. I called up a coach I knew, and asked him to consider signing me.

"Well, I don't know, Leonard, you're pretty old now." I was thirty-two. I was devastated, because I still thought I could play. In fact, I *knew* I could.

I remember the first time I went to an NFL game as a spectator after leaving the game. It was a Panthers game. Boy, did I feel like an outsider. At least I didn't have to purchase my ticket online, but I did sit with the fans. I never considered myself to be a fan; I was the game! *Those fans can't do what I can!* Wait…I mean they can't do what I *could*. That's when I realized that, not only was I not in the locker room, but I just didn't belong there anymore.

My body had clearly transitioned, but my mind had not. For me, this was tough to accept because I'd spent most of my life being a part of a sports team. I dedicated my life to a game I loved, to provide a better life for my family and to be known for doing something that most people only dreamed of doing. I did not have a clear idea as to what the next step in my life journey was going to be. I knew that I had a wife at home and a young daughter, so I had to figure this transition process out quickly.

*Transition: the word itself evokes emotions of stress, anxiety and struggle. Transition is often a good thing, but its educational processes can test a man to his limits. It can devastate and expose the fragility of men. Beware that change, especially unplanned forward and lateral movement, has left many a man beaten and in despair. I know many who have died, committed suicide, gotten hooked on drugs and alcohol, and resorted to theft because the transition to a "normal life" was too hard. Transition in and from the NFL has produced carnage, bankruptcy, and divorce; I wanted to make sure I would not be among its casualties.*
*—Eugene Robinson, 16-year NFL veteran*

There is a lot to learn from the stories of athletes transitioning from the locker room to the real world. There are many people who spiraled into depression, blew all their money, got stuck, and retreated.

But mixed in with those who struggled are the stories of men and women who transitioned in amazing ways; they may have stumbled early, but they got up, and used the skills they learned as athletes to succeed in life. I want to tell you both of these kinds of stories, and along the way, we'll talk about how to use your faith, motivation, self-assessments, core beliefs, your environment, self-talk, and your network of people to illuminate the dreams you didn't know you had, and light a path to your future.

We all have our heroes, some of whom might be athletes, whose tales of overcoming adversity and succeeding against all odds inspire us every time they step onto the field. I want the stories of athletes who have succeeded beyond the locker room to help inspire you as well.

My transition after the NFL was definitely not smooth or flawless. I had many dark nights of the soul, looking out of my office window and praying to God that I would find the right path. But during my journey, I've learned many lessons and spoken with many experts about change and success, and will share in this book what I've learned. As a personal and executive coach for individuals and businesses, I work with people every day to identify where they are in their transition mentally and emotionally, and where they want to go.

Consider this book a roadmap. Let's drill down and make sure that you are aware of the steps in transition, so you can prepare for what is to come. This book will challenge you to transform by filtering outside influences, tuning in to your inner voice, establishing purposeful goals, and dealing with doubt and fear.

In this book, we'll consider your past, evaluate your present, and help you envision a future.

*A PERSON WITHOUT A VISION IS A PERSON WITHOUT A FUTURE. AND THE PERSON WITHOUT A FUTURE WILL ALWAYS RETURN TO THEIR PAST.*

*—Edwin Lewis Cole*

In 1995, Charlotte Smith won the Best Female College Basketball Player ESPY, and she went on to play in the WNBA for 11 years. Smith experienced her own designed transition:

> *My college coach used to always tell us the six P's: Prior proper planning prevents poor performance. These words still ring true today. When I was thinking about my transition from the pros to life after sports, it was a very scary thought. I had never really ventured much outside the realm of sports. I knew that I was still passionate about the game. I never thought I'd be giving up so soon, but God was tugging at my heart for me to release it and trust Him. Too often, we allow what we do to define who we are.*
>
> *The latter part of my pro career, I started to realize that I was getting the coaching bug, so I began collecting all of my playbooks from all the teams I'd played for, so I could use them as references. I continued to pay close attention to the details of teaching drills. I started taking notes after each practice about how the drill was taught. I also started reading a lot of motivational books and books about leadership. John Maxwell is one of my favorite authors. I am also big into writing. I journal a lot so I keep a log on what has transpired in my life. People will always want to hear your journey because of your sports background.*
>
> *But my transition was pretty seamless as I had already positioned myself to become an assistant coach. The last four years of my professional career in basketball, I opted not to go play overseas during the offseason but to coach as an assistant at my alma mater, the University of North Carolina. It was a sacrifice, as I could have made more money continuing to play professionally, but I knew that this temporary sacrifice would get me where I needed to be in the long run. I currently serve as the Head Coach at Elon University!*

PRIOR PROPER PLANNING WILL ALWAYS
PREVENT POOR PERFORMANCE.

## Part One: Locker Rooms of the Past

In this section, we'll look back to our childhoods to see how we were influenced by our identity, values, and training to become the people we are today. Who you were growing up is tremendously important to understanding what dreams you left behind, what values you had, and the strengths you found in training that now may be lacking in your life. These issues are all important to moving forward with the transitions in our lives.

**Chapter One:**

## WHO ARE YOU? IDENTIFYING
## CORE BELIEFS ABOUT YOURSELF

*By the time Lisa was ten years old, everyone knew she was fast and that track and field could take her far. Her parents knew, her teachers knew, her friends knew, and her coaches absolutely knew that she was a star. As she developed and got older, Lisa couldn't really go anywhere without someone mentioning something about track. When she was at school, her teachers asked about her upcoming meets in order to make adjustments to her workload and assignments for class. At practice, her coaches pushed her hard and insisted on her absolute best, telling her that a college scholarship was at stake. At lunch, in the hallways, and after school, her friends expressed envy at different levels—some wishing they could actually be her, and others wishing they could merely experience the notable adulation brought on by her athletic ability.*

*Lisa liked all the attention, and assumed that track must have been what made her special, so she submitted to the hype and eventually embraced it. Thoughts she had about being anything other than a sprinter were fleeting, mostly because she didn't seem to have time or any support from adults, who celebrated focus and concentration on track.*

Who we are, and who others perceive us to be, is often identified when we are babies and toddlers: mischievous, quiet, happy, angry, shy. As we get older, we might be identified by our reputation in the classroom as the class clown, smart, teacher's pet, or slow-to-learn. Out on the playing field we might be known as a fast runner, strong, a great kicker—or the one no one wanted on their team. People like to label, and those labels can stick.

My aunt gave my nickname—Tink—when I was little. It was a nickname that stuck with me throughout my years growing up. My high school coaches even called me Tink, and to this day, when I return home to Toccoa, Georgia, to visit my parents and be with all my family, everyone calls me Tink. Nicknames help bring you back to understanding of who you are—just like going back to your childhood home does. Mine continues to keep me connected to my community, where no one calls me Leonard, but everyone calls me Tink. They even awarded me Hall of Fame honors this year, which totally humbles me.

A nickname can also serve as an intimidator: my NFL roommate with the Bengals, Darryl Williams, had the nickname Hit Man, because when he was in college he used to knock people out as a defensive player. He carried that nickname throughout his years in the NFL. You didn't want to be on offense knowing that a guy called Hit Man was ready to knock your lights out. (He is also the godfather of my daughter, just in case she ends up with someone I don't particularly like…Just kidding!)

But what do labels do for us? They can be fun, but they can also be limiting.

Ever wonder why an athlete, labeled a jock, who is also articulate and does really well in the classroom seems like such a shock to people? Because his identity has been tied to his sport. This becomes dangerous to a young athlete's future when he is not given the opportunity to explore interests beyond sports. Often an athlete does not have the support needed to develop talents outside of the ones needed for his sport—like speed, strength, agility, and ball-handling skills.

Alternatively, think about a child whose parents want her to become a doctor. They talk about her being a doctor. They talk to other people in the child's presence about her becoming a doctor. They enroll the child in math and science programs. They even take the child to visit schools that have stellar medical programs. How hard would it be for this child to nurture authentic aspirations of being a guitarist in a band? How hard would it be for the child to really conceptualize any unrelated identity, other than that which had been set out before her? Pretty hard, I'm sure.

People compete with others' ideas of them, without knowing for sure who they really are. Athletes and other talented people have to have the presence of mind to move through their environments, fully aware that they are more than the NOW, because there is more life to live beyond sport, fame, success, and temporary labels.

It's crazy to compete with the perceptions of others without first being honest with yourself about who you really are. Some people want to prove the opposite of what others think about them, and other people, who are not aware of their influencing factors, simply believe what others say and live up to the hype. We have all seen that player who grew up on the farm and emerged from some rural athletic program lose his/her values when they make it to the pros. All of a sudden fast cars, VIP status, jewelry, and accumulating other material items becomes the priority. However, the truth is, this person is family-oriented, grew up in church, and rotated five or six outfits all year without complaining. Yes, this is an extreme example, but the subtleties in this lesson ring true for many people with regard to self-image and identity.

Sometimes you have to be stronger than your reality.

My stutter started when I was a kid. I stuttered all the way into college. This had a huge effect on me: I was scared to answer questions in class or raise my hand in case I stuttered in front of everybody. Not answering questions can make you feel like you're not smart enough, because others think you don't know the answers. So even though you know you're smart, you can start internalizing how others perceive you and then start living it out.

I became the punchline of many jokes and got laughed at. A lot. But athletics was one of those things that kept me connected to my confidence and sense of self-worth. When I was feeling insecure, being good at something on the field or the court allowed me to feel competent. Being a part of my team and having other people reliant on me helped me not focus on my stuttering. My mom was always another confidence builder, filling my head with love and encouraging words.

In the ninth grade on the first day of basketball practice, Coach Snell had us go around the group and tell our names and the position we played in front of everyone on the team. I was so scared. I thought maybe if I silently said the name "Leonard Wheeler" in my head over and over again, it would not be a problem when my turn came to speak. Finally, it was my turn, "My name is Len...Len... Len...Len... " I stuttered my butt off. From then on, every other time Coach would see me, he'd say, " Hi Len-Len-Len-Leonard Wheeler." That reminded me of that embarrassing moment, but I used that humiliation as leverage to make myself better at things. When I started playing defense in high school and spotted those people who had laughed at me, it was *Game On!*

I got to where I was laughing at myself, thinking "You're going to start getting a seizure if you don't stop stuttering." But when it affected my relationship with high school girlfriends, ugh—that was just embarrassing.

My final straw came one night when I was a senior in college. I was in my dorm room, praying. I had to take a speech class for my business major, and I worried I was going to be completely humiliated in front of everybody when I would inevitably start to stutter. But amazingly, that was the last night I ever had a problem with compulsive stuttering. I attribute my success in overcoming that speech problem to this: when you become intentional about the things you want, you get what you focus on. When I was focusing on the fear of stuttering and the bitterness I felt from getting teased, I was only going to get more of that from myself and other people. I have always believed that God answers prayers. He truly answered mine.

*Do not be anxious about anything, but in*
*everything by prayer and supplication with thanksgiving*
*let your request be made known to God*

*—Philippians 4:6*

We all have issues and problems that we have to overcome. Some of these things are not necessarily problems that other people can see and hear, but we know what they are. We have to make the conscious effort that it's not going to continue to rule us.

It might seem ironic that now I make my living from my ability to convey ideas and information clearly and effectively. People are shocked when I go home, and they hear me speak with no stutter. They can't believe it's me speaking so clearly.

> *For God did not give us a spirit of fear*
> *but of power and love and self control.*
>                                    — *2 Timothy 1:7*

But the past humiliations with stuttering sometimes continue to stoke me—it's a way that I use different challenges in my life without allowing them to render me ineffective. That's one of the keys: to use past success *and* failures to propel you forward. But if you can't use a bad memory to push yourself into forward action, then stop reminding yourself, and let that memory go.

Take a moment to think about how you would characterize yourself. Now, think about how much of that characterization comes from your own authentic spirit—that voice way down deep inside of you. How is that different from what people have told you about yourself? It is certainly possible for others to affirm what you think, but it is a different thing altogether for you to allow others to shape your thoughts about yourself. We would be more alarmed if the influence was negative, right?

Let's take a relationship between a man and a woman, where the man is constantly commenting on the weight of his partner, even though she is a normal size. Since she values the relationship, she internalizes his criticism. He comments on her weight over and over and over again, suggesting she go to the gym more often, or go on a diet. By the time their relationship is over, the damage is done. This woman now has body image issues, but no one can understand why. Most of us would have a negative opinion about the man in this situation, but at the same time wish that the woman had the wherewithal to not internalize "his" issue. Because she was not in touch with her inner self, she was unable to move on without making his issues her own.

Now let's take a look at another situation. A student athlete, raised by a single mother, has a male teacher he is very close to. This teacher is always telling the player that he'd better hurry up and complete his work or he will be late for practice, that he's good enough to make it to the pros, and that he is the best athlete the school has seen in years. This respected teacher continuously makes these comments and stays close to the student athlete. What the student athlete internalizes is: *I am good at sports.* This is positive. However, what the teacher is *not* saying has profound impact on the student athlete as well. The teacher never gives any positive feedback about the quality of his schoolwork, his educational interests or strengths, nor does the athlete receive any mention of his ability to do well at anything else other than sports. As an impressionable individual, the student athlete quite naturally focuses on athletics because of the encouragement he receives from a respected person in his life. To further affirm this path, the coach, his mother, and his peers chime in as well, with the same tune. It is no wonder why he may not be so inclined to explore other areas: he has not been given the social license or support to do so.

We can get caught up in an identity, and that identity can sometimes create something that's sustainably good, or sustainably bad. In school, you don't have to belong to just one group. I know athletes who are geeks. A center who played for the Minnesota Vikings graduated from Yale and was a great football player. Don't buy into any "this is who I am" mentality, because we are all more-than-one-dimensional—but at the same time, never think that being an athlete is bad.

Transition is about you being able to cross over into different areas that sometimes are seen as outside of what is the norm—but that's OK. You have to learn to create your new norm.

## Your Identity

How do you view your place in the world—what do you want to get out of it and what do you believe you are purposed to give back? In my work with athletes and business owners, I have met many who are financially secure, had successful careers, a great family, fanfare, and more friends than they can count. Yet some of these individuals are miserable. They chased the spoils of life that the rest of the world thought they should have, like cars, houses, jewelry, and exotic vacations. I am not saying that all of those things aren't great to have. They are true enhancements to anyone's life, including mine. But the truth is, it's impossible to be truly happy or content without thinking or believing in what is inherently inside of you. There is something bigger than what we possess externally.

Look at pictures of yourself growing up. See how the transitions happened. You might have started loving Legos, or video games, or animals. You wanted to be a vet, an actor, a pilot, a soldier, a fireman or policeman. What changed you in your outlook? Did you think those dreams were childish, or out of the realm of possibility? Look at your early years like a movie: is it a comedy, a drama, an action or a feel-good movie? How do you feel when you look back on your life and view it? It has a lot to do with the choices you make moving forward. You can see and dwell on the bad parts, or you can see it as a triumph.

If I see a picture of myself when I was little, it's hard to believe I grew up to become a professional football player.

I was a small, skinny kid from the projects of Toccoa, Georgia, where, in the 80s, we faced a lot of racial tension. For a small kid in the projects, there weren't a whole lot of visible opportunities to make it big. My mom and dad divorced when I was ten. I had that stutter. There didn't seem to be a whole lot of hope in that picture, and yet I'm still thriving.

The greatest gift is love, and that's what I received in the midst of not having a lot of vision of how my life could be different. My mom, sisters, brothers, stepdad, aunts, uncles, and real friends helped me to believe that God's will for me doesn't have to be limited to what I can see. Hebrews 11:1 is a scripture that I live my life by every day: *Now faith is the substance of things hoped for, the evidence of things not seen.* I wore this scripture on my hip in every football game I played in my senior year at Troy University. I believe that our Father in Heaven doesn't always allow us to see everything that is purposed for us when we desire to see it, but it's always on time.

## Your Environment

Do you believe that environment always wins? It's impossible not to be influenced by the environment in which you were raised. The people, the culture, and the atmosphere around you influenced your life views. Parents, siblings, friends, coaches, and teachers directly or indirectly pressured you to be who *they* wanted you to be.

For many who have carried the expectations of others for years, unraveling all of those layers takes time and work. We have to identify the outside influences and deconstruct them, then commit ourselves to filtering other influences in the future to stay true to our core identity. Even if you didn't before, try being purposefully present now: conscious of the people and messages around you that have the power to impact how you see yourself. Also understand that you may have internalized too much of those outside influences in the past, and because of that, you feel attached to your current title.

Hardy Nickerson, current linebacker coach for the Tampa Bay Buccaneers, played sixteen seasons in the NFL. He says:

*From my parents, I learned the value of hard work, account-ability, and consistency. Watching my dad as a child, I saw a man who never missed a day of work. He was a 'no frills' type of guy who worked extremely hard, was proud of his hard work, and was someone you could rely on and count on. He made it a point to make sure I understood that hard work pays off. He also emphasized being competitive and putting out your best work in everything you do.*

I had a different type of experience where I grew up in Georgia. There was definitely a poverty mindset growing up that people found very difficult to fight against. It seemed like no one ever left the projects. The environment doesn't have to be negative, but if your negative environment wins, you can become bitter, hateful, and even resentful. My mother made sure that I would think of the world beyond the one I was in as a world of opportunity. Please take every chance you get to say thank you to the people who have sown seeds in your life to assist you to this point.

## The Power of Thought

*As a man thinketh so is he.*

—*Proverbs 23:7*

*To take that a step further, as a man thinketh—so he does.*

Parents often want their kids to try lots of activities—from sports to the arts, to see what will resonate with them, to see what they will become passionate about. However, most professional athletes don't have the same luxury growing up today, as they are now focused from an early age on just one or two sports, to perfect their gift.

Hardy Nickerson wanted to go to law school after college.

*I always felt like If I wasn't going to play football very long, then I wanted to go to law school and someday practice law. As it turned out, I was able to play for sixteen years in the NFL, which far exceeded the four-year career I was hoping for as a rookie in 1987. It was important at the time to think realistically about my other interests and goals in case pro football did not work out. However, I ended up playing for almost two decades, which obviously changed my outlook and path for other interests.*

Some people have tunnel vision around an athlete's physical gift, and don't put energy into helping them do the necessary work to develop in other areas. So an athlete can go years and years focusing on only one element of themselves, until the moment where it all comes to an end and the void sets in. No sports. No practice. No teammates, no locker room, and no real structure can equal failure. It is indeed scary to get to this point where the void is ever-present, the core beliefs about who you are have been mostly an outsider's opinion, and you have nothing else to latch onto. This state of mind at times is inevitable. Accept that your focus on sports served you well for a certain period in your life, and now is the opportunity to focus on something else that you did not choose or seriously consider in your earlier stages of life.

Each transition in life is a building block—but now is the point when YOU get to decide what you're building on, and what to leave in the past. We need to establish a solid foundation and then build so that we can sustain success.

**Journal:**

This section in each chapter is here to assist you in learning more about yourself, and will help direct you where to go.

Think back to your own background. As you were exposed to different people, value systems, belief systems, and environments, what influenced you—for good and bad? Some things may only stick with you for a period of time, and other things may have become of part of your identity for a longer period of time, but it's important to reflect on when and where we picked up small elements of our identity.

Who are/were the important people in your life who influenced you along the way?

_____

_____

_____

_____

_____

What messages did they send to you (directly or indirectly) about who you would become? Be specific.

_____

_____

_____

_____

_____

Did you have any dreams or goals that you did not pursue when you were a kid, for whatever reason? What were they?

_____

_____

_____

_____

Did you have a nickname, or were you labeled as a certain type? How did that influence you and your development, good or bad?

_____

_____

_____

_____

## Chapter Two:

## LIFE LESSONS LEARNED ON TEAMS

*I took every stimulus thrown my way to prepare for my future, post-NFL. The meetings, the regulated schedule, the discipline to be on time and attentive were constant and easy to adhere to. The working within a team fabric, the submission to authority, learning to compromise, the interpersonal relationships, handling stress, wins, losses, happiness, anger, working out conflicts...In football, you are trying to make right decisions within a span of 1.5 seconds, only to do it over and over again in a 60-minute contest, with someone trying to outsmart you physically and mentally. All of it taught me and prepared me for the next phase of life. I was able to take advantage of the opportunities afforded me. I was on the lookout for change (transition) because football is a precarious sport. The NFL's nature, its DNA, is built on change—change in position, game plan, team, personnel, options, and the like. One day you are in, then suddenly you're out. It's just that abrupt.*

*—Eugene Robinson*

If there is one thing athletes know well, it's structure. We had to study, learn the playbook, practice, weight train, attend team meetings. We had to eat right, sleep enough, get extra coaching, and run drills. When you're a professional athlete, your days during the season and in training are regimented like the armed forces.

I might be biased (OK, I almost certainly am, so if football is not your game, just take this with a grain of salt), but I can't think of another sport besides football that teaches its players so many life skills. I have played basketball and run track, but football has so many more pieces to it than those sports. Football requires play-by-play talks around strategy. As a team, we're constantly communicating. I coached my daughter in soccer and those girls always had to communicate and think strategy the entire game as well. OK, OK, OK...*all* sports are significant in our developmental stages mentally, socially, and emotionally. Parents, please encourage your kid to play a sport.

Any type of team you can think of should be in the process of constantly communicating, regrouping, and trying all over again. This should happen with your family, your mentors, your friends, your colleagues, and your classmates. Sometimes we are open to receiving information and using that information to be successful. Sometimes we're not open, and it shows in the results.

Let's take a look at the lessons we learn as players on teams, and how those skills can be used as we make our transitions in life. If you weren't on a team, it's useful to see how the discipline of training affects the athlete; you can apply these lessons in almost any field.

### Show Up On Time

Being an athlete on any level means you had to show up at a certain place at a certain time in order for the team to witness your commitment. You have to show up for practice and show up for meetings (even the ones you don't consider important), or risk the consequences.

Showing up on time is key in every facet of life—school, your job, a date, a doctor's appointment.

The tenet that I live by goes like this: showing up exactly on time means you're focused on being late. Because you can have one of two intentions when you have an appointment: either to be late, or to be early. If you're doing things at the last minute and still tying your shoes on the way in the door, your life is all about rushing and procrastinating. I believe that being late is totally disrespectful and implies entitlement. The way you do some things is usually the way you do most. Rushing and being late is going to show up somewhere else. Negative habits like this hold you hostage and create emotional chaos. You never feel prepared. Regardless of all the work you've done up to that point, the emotion takes over and you're just not ready. I prefer to be prepared, not rushed, and not off my game.

One day in 1993, when I was playing for the Cincinnati Bengals, was the first and only time I was ever late to our facility. It was the day before a game. You should *never* be late the day before a game. I was living over the border in Kentucky, and commuting to Cincinnati via a bridge from Kentucky to Ohio. I had no idea that the bridge that I needed to cross was closed. There were four of us in our cars following one another, and we all panicked. On the detour, we started running red lights, and taking the back roads to get around the backlogged traffic. That group of us walked into the locker room two minutes late, and the looks we got from every team member and then the head coach said: *You'd better not have a bad game*, and, *I'm sorry our big game wasn't important enough for you to be on time.*

Your integrity is important. Your team needs to know you can be counted on to be there on time for them. If you disregard people by always being late, it's unacceptable to them, and should be unacceptable to you. You are being selfish and disrespectful, and you will be called on it. Abraham Lincoln once said, "You can fool all the people some of the time, and some of the people all the time, but you cannot fool all the people all the time."

Do everything you can to show up five minutes early to every meeting. Be OK with being the first person on a conference call or in the room. Celebrities and athletes have a bad rap for showing up to most events late. It is not acceptable on any level, and if you start asking around, you will hear the lack of tolerance toward people who are late. If people are allowing you to get away with being late, are you really getting away with anything? You are digging a hole for yourself because you're setting unrealistic expectations on your value; you're going to think that everyone will allow your selfish behavior.

Change your behavior and stop setting yourself up to fail over and over.

## Teamwork

When geese fly in a V formation, they increase their flight range by 71 percent because each bird is flying slightly above the bird in front of it. When the lead goose gets tired, it goes to the back to rest and another takes its place; that way the group shares flight fatigue. The V formation also allows the geese to communicate more effectively and to see every other goose. The accountability is amazing. The energy that it would take for geese to fly to another state alone would prove to be detrimental to their wings and heart rate. Who taught them to do that? It's a learned behavior that demands that each bird be accountable to the others in the group.

Teams help us to rely on others to do their part. Everyone has an assignment that affects the rest of the team. Being on a team teaches us not to try to pursue everything in our lives on our own. Mentorships are built because someone has already gone through the fire, the rough patches, so you don't have to make the same mistakes or experience the same pitfalls as they did. Every team has veterans on it, and those veterans help nurture and cultivate their younger teammates. This process should happen in sports, in business, and in life.

I grew up in a small community where everyone invested in everyone else's children. My mom would tell the other adults in our neighborhood that they could discipline me if they witnessed me doing something bad when she wasn't around. It takes a village to raise a child, goes the adage, and that was certainly true in our neighborhood. On a team, coaches and players help keep the others in line, because they know if there is one weak link, at some point the whole team will suffer.

## Be Accountable

Being accountable is not about just showing up, it's about promising to practice your part so you can win—not just for your sake, but also for your teammates'. Without a true value system, it's hard to understand what to be accountable to and why. For me, God's word defines the alignment of accountability.

I have experienced times when my level of accountability wasn't up to par, and it showed in my performance every time. I had to learn to be accountable to myself, which then allowed me to be accountable to other people. You have to beware of your pride and your ego for you to be able to receive a high level of accountability from others. Hidden pride and ego will usually make you think you possess all the answers.

*My high school football coach repeatedly explained to us what his definition of discipline was: the ability to carry out an arduous task over and over again, and having the ability to control any situation we were placed in. When I look back, there are so many people and things that contributed to helping me achieve success. However, the things that stick out the most were: hard work, being accountable, being consistent, and being disciplined.*

*—Hardy Nickerson*

## Compete to Play

You don't automatically get to play on the field or the court. You have to show the coaches that there's a good reason why they should put you in.

Why should the coach trust a person enough to be the team leader? Why should the coach trust you to have the ball on the last play when they haven't seen you perform with a level of consistency that warrants what you desire? Why should or did your coach trust you?

Being out on the field and the court can sometimes be good

enough for some. I think a lot of people are satisfied with just being in the game. But what about being involved, making plays, and helping your team win? Are you living more by your words, or more by your actions? Is your team following you because of what you're saying, or what you're doing? Or both? If you're stepping up, I commend you. If you're not, it's time for you to stop being a spectator in your own game.

When I was in the eighth grade, I didn't get to play a lot in the football games, even though I felt like I was a good player. My confidence level didn't match my talent. In the ninth grade, I didn't play, even though my confidence level matched my talent. I found my position in the tenth grade from Coach Cox, my high school coach. He came over and saw me practicing as an offensive lineman (yes I said, *offensive* lineman), and saw I was fast and aggressive. He recognized that I could be a good defensive back. I was stunned, and thought, "What, I can hit people my size, and not two times my size? This is going to be fun!" Don't be afraid to compete when given the opportunity.

When my high school retired my football jersey, my ninth grade coach was there, and said, "Well, that just shows how much I knew! I had him playing on the offensive line." I liked his honesty. He had the humility to know that you're not always going to have everything figured out—and it's never too late to change direction.

## Is the Coach King?

When you're on a team, what the coach thinks about you and how he or she directs you is extremely important. In a lot of instances, it will dictate the direction of your high school and college experiences.

I've had coaches I didn't like, but it didn't change the fact that I had to play within their system. I had to play for the team, regardless of my own dislikes. I signed up to be a team player.

How do you play for someone you don't respect? This will help when you transition for your work life. Chances are pretty good that you're going to not like someone you report to, or you may have colleagues you don't agree with. So how can you get past your own dislikes, judgments, and biases? You get past it by remembering to play for the cause—the win, the deal, the promotion, the why—and not for the specific person who is rubbing you the wrong way.

In youth athletics, I have often seen parents with a jarring attitude toward coaches, parents who try to influence the coach to give their child more playing time regardless of their son or daughter's abilities. Parents, back off, and let the coach coach. Players, regardless of what mom and dad might say, the world is not just about you. Get rid of the idea that your parents are the ones who run your team. They are simply getting in the way of the *coach* running the team. If the coach is not a good coach, there is usually a hierarchical process to pursue with your complaint. A coach who is afraid of parents and allows them to influence his or her decisions will never be a strong coach for the entire team, unless the influence is positive and makes sense.

A successful coach rewards those who show their best side, not their worst. Parents, if you feel the coach is not fair, ask for a private meeting with them to discuss your kid.

Look at your patterns of behavior, and ask yourself, *Is this how I want to be for the rest of my life?* Putting yourself and your needs first all the time is a dead end. You're going to find out one day that you do not know how to deal with people on your own, or handle life's difficulties. One day your parents are not going to be there to rescue you. Wake up! You are a leader. It's time to display your leadership abilities and step up to be a better team player. You are now your own internal coach. What you continue to tell yourself about you will become your norm. This self-talk will continually build your foundational leadership belief system.

### Sacrifice

Part of being on a team is accepting that you are probably not going to get to play in the position that you wanted to play. You may have to take an unpopular position in order to play. After all, there can only be one quarterback.

One day I got a phone call from a friend of mine. His son was upset about what his assignment was on his team: "Our son wants to play running back, but the coach wants him to play center." This little guy was nine. They put him on the phone to talk to me about it.

"Hey, Mr. Wheeler."

"Hi, John. How's it going at football practice?" "Good, except they want me to play center. I don't want to play center."

"Why don't you want to play center?" I asked.

"I don't want someone touching my butt," he said.

I tried not to laugh, because his feelings were valid. "John," I said, "I wouldn't want people touching my butt either, bud. But do you think your coach has given that role to you because he trusts you? You're the first person to hold the football in a play. If you don't snap it right to the quarterback, your team doesn't have a chance to win. Can you see how important that is?"

"Yes sir."

"John, I want you to practice hard and be the best center that your coach has ever seen. And then you might be able to play running back. It's not going to be popular, and you might not like it— but you're the best at it. You're the first one to touch the ball because the coach trusts you."

I heard a few weeks later that John did great, and was indeed given the role of running back later in the season. But he didn't automatically get it—he had to prove himself to the coach. Oh, and another thing? He was MVP.

People tell me all the time that they want to be successful, and then I ask them, "What are you willing to sacrifice?" It's easy to desire greatness, wealth, and fame, and when we see other individuals attain it, we judge and automatically think it was easy. We see the finished product and not the hard work behind closed doors.

What are you willing to sacrifice?

## Self-Discipline

When you play on a team, you don't get to go home after school during the season. There's practice—lots of practice, and then you still have to do your homework once you do get home. You miss out on relaxing after school, and watching some dumb TV show you love, or playing a video game. You are sacrificing your free time for something greater than your wants.

Former NBA player Dale Davis shares about a time in high school when his self-discipline kicked in, almost too late.

*It was our senior year and I was fortunate to hang with some good guys who had athletic talent. We were going on our senior trip to Panama Beach to do the usual stuff like hang out, party, and look for girls. I had a scholarship at Clemson, and I had to report back to school earlier than the other guys. They said they would bring me back early, but I wasn't sure about it. The fun crew showed up at my house and said, "You're going," and they threw my stuff in a garbage bag for the trip. These guys all understood what my scholarship meant to me, but they still pushed me over the edge of my caution. So I went with them.*

*Most of our self-esteem came from our teams. As black athletes from the projects in the south, we had to stick together socially. The team mentality would follow us and protect us. So I felt the pressure when the guys said, "You're going."*

*On the field or the court, we were different animals than we were when we were home. Home was the projects; there was nothing good about it except it was our home. A lot of athletes had the premonition that if we could make it in sports, we could pave the way for ourselves and for our families who helped us get there.*

*I got in the car with my garbage bag of clothes. I had less than five dollars in my pocket. Everyone was happy; the music was playing, the car rolling along toward a fun time. Suddenly a feeling came over me. "Stop," I said.*

*"Stop? What did you forget?"*

*"Nothing," I said. "Didn't forget nothing. I can't go. I have to report to Clemson."*

*I think we were all in shock as the car stopped, two miles into the journey. Right then and there, I not only saw my future, I felt it, and it was more important to me than fun; it was more important to me than anything in the world. I started walking and never looked back. I think in that moment, as bad as I felt about missing the trip, I walked toward a future vision. Even though I didn't know the details, I knew exactly where I was walking.*

Dale Davis walked right into the 1991 NBA Draft and was a first-round pick for the Indiana Pacers. He played in the NBA for sixteen years with the Pacers, the Trail Blazers, the Golden State Warriors, and the Pistons.

Dale's story speaks of the self-discipline that is required when your vision for the future is bigger than the temporary fun of today. He is not saying don't enjoy your life, but he is saying *understand the risk and make sure that you measure the cost for every action.* Dale was a great student in school, and just so happened to be a great basketball player as well. Dale is now a successful businessman living in Atlanta, Georgia.

### How to Win and Lose Gracefully

From the time you play your first game of Candyland, you quickly learn you're not going to win every game. Back when you were little, you might have upended the game board and run out of the room, furious that you lost. Well, as you get bigger, you can't do that anymore. You have to learn sportsmanship. You learn how to shake your opponents' hands before and after the game. You have to take a defeat with grace and not storm off the field, and you also have to celebrate a win in such a way that is not cruel to those who lost.

For sportsmanship, look at the Miami Heat and the San Antonio Spurs for the 2014 championship series. The Heat were the defending champions, and they lost 4–1. Even though we know that it had to hurt for Lebron James to come over and shake his opponents' hands when the Spurs won, the Heat bowed out gracefully and congratulated the other team on a job well done.

In sports, we gain the most valuable lessons when we learn how to win and lose gracefully. Learn how to say, "Great job, and congratulations." Recognizing others' accomplishments is a sign of strength, not weakness.

When I went to Troy University (which was Troy State when I attended in 1991), I had one year left to play in order to get drafted into the NFL. I had transferred from Ole Miss to Troy, where I met some great players on both the offense and defense who already had established positions on the team. I knew in order to get some playing time, I would have to win a position. I did, and it had to be hard on the players who'd been working with this team for years to see some guy transfer from another school and claim a position. Yet they were able to not only show me respect, but became my great friends.

Later that year, I ended up getting drafted into the NFL's third round. I wanted so badly for my new teammates, who had become some of my best friends, to get drafted as well. But when they didn't, they were amazingly gracious to me as they watched me going to a place we had all dreamed of playing as kids. They showed me how to win with how they treated me, regardless of how difficult it might have been for them.

### Playing with People You Don't Like

What I love about sports is that it involves individuals from every walk of life. A sport is the only activity in which you can be in a war with another country and compete against them while displaying great sportsmanship and respect—look at the players in the World Cup, or the Olympics. Players' differences in culture allow for great conversations.

When I played Pee Wee, middle school, high school, college,

and professional football, I never witnessed everyone getting along singing "Kumbaya," because it's not reality. People will rub you the wrong way for inane reasons—like the way they eat gets on your last nerve—or profound reasons, like being a racist, or a misogynist, or a bully. But when you're on a team together, you have to rise above the personal dislikes and focus on the end game, which is winning as a team (or in some cases, just winning).

Some of your most competitive opponents will be and are your best friends. I played against my best friends for years, and I even found myself playing harder against them than against the people I didn't like on my own team. Of course sometimes you're not going to like your opponent. You're conditioned to see them as a mythical enemy, even though they're just as human as you. This disassociating with somebody else's humanity allows us to hit hard, outrun, defend, and score for our side.

This same theory is applicable to life in the corporate sector. If you worked for Nike and your best friend worked for Reebok, there would be a little tension if you were both pursuing the same big account. We have to continue engaging in the friendly fire of competition during our transition. In your new job, you're probably not going to like everyone you work with, but you must respect them as teammates and win for the whole and not just for the sum of its parts.

## The Code of the Locker Room

I have been in a lot of different locker rooms over the past thirty-nine years of my life, since the age of six. (I think I just gave away my age, but let's stay focused here, can we?)

The locker room is a safe haven, a place of trust and transparency, a place of hiding, a place of planning, a sacred place, a place where you build, a scary place, and a place of reflection. The locker room is a lot like your home. It is a place where you can become or begin. When you walk into the locker room, it shifts your mindset from one dimension to another. I doubt if every approach into the locker room was or is ever the same on a daily basis, but one thing is constant: you start every game and practice being in the locker room first. Your self-talk is key when in the locker room because it creates your performance state of mind. You will actually play the game in your head before you play the game. When you stand up to walk out for the game, you transform into the role you play on the field. You communicate this to yourself with your thoughts as you motivate yourself to win and play your best. You convince yourself of what you have to accomplish in order to be successful. As you walk to the field or court, you are *becoming*.

Conversely, when the game is over, and you pass back through the locker room, you become "yourself" again. Your transition can be intentional: shedding your previous persona and taking on a new one. Some will learn it with grace while others will struggle, making the same mistakes over and over, acting as if they were still on the same team, playing the same game, or driven by the results of athletic endeavors. Some will be depressed, missing the good things while escalating the bad times to "memories" instead of lessons. We have to trust that we have a team of people around us and that we aren't on this transition journey alone.

People will attempt to make you feel as if you're just a "regular person" in your transition, but the truth be told, God doesn't make regular people. People choose to feel regular, then they start to live out how they feel. Psalm 139:14 says: *I will give thanks to You, for I am fearfully and wonderfully made; Wonderful are Your works, And my soul knows it very well.*

IT IS IMPORTANT FOR YOU TO KNOW WHO YOU ARE,
OR YOU WILL BECOME WHO OTHERS SAY YOU ARE.

The code of the locker room has taught me the importance of transformation before I play the game of life. We have to sometimes change our clothes for the part. We have to make sure that we have the right equipment. We have to look across and see who's playing on our team and in the game with us. We have to be prepared to call an audible and adapt to the unknown while learning to anticipate the next move.

The locker room was special because real connection and camaraderie occurred there, and life-long relationships were cultivated. Take the lessons you learned there forward into your next phase of life, and fill up your new mental locker room with the equipment and relationships you need to be successful in your phase of life.

*The thing I enjoyed most about playing in the NFL was the competition and the camaraderie you could develop among teammates. I really liked the challenge of being pushed to be your best every weekend against the best players in the world. That really pushed me beyond what I even I thought I could do. I also enjoyed the sense of camaraderie I had with teammates, and the sense that we had each others' backs. The constant interaction with teammates fostered a sense of brotherhood and kinship unlike anything else.*
                                        —*Hardy Nickerson, 16 year NFL pro*

**Journal:**

What lessons from teamwork have you experienced?

_____
_____
_____
_____
_____
_____

Who are you accountable to? Why?

_____
_____
_____
_____
_____

How many times have you been accountable to the wrong person?

_____

_____

_____

_____

_____

_____

On a scale of 1 to 10, where 1 means you feel that others are responsible for what you do and what happens to you, and where 10 means that you are entirely responsible for what you do and what happens to you, what's your level of accountability for your own actions?

_____

_____

_____

_____

_____

_____

_____

What are you willing to sacrifice to be successful?

_____

_____

_____

_____

_____

_____

_____

_____

## Chapter Three:

## TEENAGERS, LISTEN UP!

Every individual who has ever played a sport had a dream of going and playing on a bigger stage, be it high school, college, or the pros. While that doesn't always happen, the desire to achieve that goal is just as powerful whether it is reached or not.

Why is the *thought* of taking the action just as powerful? It is the thought of not completing the course or finishing the race that slows down our transformation cycle.

> *Do you not know that in a race all the runners run, but only one gets the prize? Run in such a way as to get the prize.*
> —*1 Corinthians 9:24.*

Why is finishing so important in during transforming? When we finish something, we create a mindset that wants to complete and celebrate the small victories. Completion becomes habitual, which then allows us to see a positive outcome of our actions. We might have a conversation with ourselves or others that sounds like this: *I'm not good enough to go on to college and play, but I'm totally OK with that.* Or, *The only colleges that wanted me to play for them were small schools, so I decided not to play anymore.* Or, *I'm not big or fast enough to play at the next level, but I'm totally cool with that.* When has a true champion ever been OK with the words *I'm totally OK with not being good enough?*

I understand that you might want to move on and forget it, but you need to deal with the disappointing things that happen to you.

It is OK to mourn over what you've experienced…even as a strong teenager.

Maybe you didn't go to that smaller school for various reasons, but at least deal with the fact that you believe that you're better than what others say and think. Your emotions over the loss of a future you once dreamed of must be dealt with now, or they will keep dragging you back to the memory graveyard. When a sport ends, for some it is a devastating loss. You might be acting as if it's just not a big deal. Really?

In this book, I deal with the realities of our feelings, and while some of my theories might be wrong for you, they will still make you think, reflect and react.

My daughter, at the time of me writing this book, is a seventeen-year-old senior in high school, a great student-athlete who runs track for Ardrey Kell High School in Charlotte, North Carolina. Lindsey grew up running and playing soccer from the age of five. But when she went into the eleventh grade, she declared that her pursuit of college sports would not involve soccer, just track. Track had become one of her passions. This conscious decision allowed her transition to be smoother than if the decision had to be made to stop soccer *and* track, because she is easing out of having both sports be a big player in her life. Now that she is down to one, she can concentrate on her academics and her running. I always tell Lindsey that academics is not the fall back plan; it's *the* plan, period.

REFLECT ON WHAT PLAYING YOUR SPORT HAS MEANT TO YOU,
AND THE TRUE VALUE THAT IT BROUGHT TO YOUR LIFE.

It is not easy to live with the regret of quitting, stopping, or just not pursuing something you love because of a lack of effort. The decision may haunt you for years if it's not dealt with appropriately and swiftly. A key element in your transformation journey is this question: *Who are you?* And don't tell me your name. Who are you? And don't tell me what you do. *Who are you?* The reason I ask this question is because for so long you were known as the lacrosse player, the soccer player, the football player, the basketball player, the volleyball player, the wrestler, the cheerleader, the gymnast, the dancer, the genius, the track star, or the kid who played sports. Who do you claim to be? Who do you desire to be? How do you voice it with real conviction and own it?

Education is everything. I tell students, "I don't care that you don't want to stay up late studying for the test. Get over it, and do it. What does that test grade represent to you ten years later, or twenty years later? It could be the difference between you and that great college you want to go to, whose reputation can get you that job you really want, or that graduate school that you've dreamed of attending."

Here are a few words from my daughter Lindsey:

*Being seventeen and a senior in high school can be intimidating at times. All of a sudden you see college and adulthood coming right around the corner a lot faster than you realized you were ready for. When you're a kid, everyone tells you that time will fly by, but let's be honest, you don't really believe them. You know high school and college will end one day, but deep inside, you believe you'll never have to actually grow up. You don't believe that one day you'll be just like your parents, worrying about paying bills, maintaining a stable job, and getting to the age where getting older isn't looked at with excitement anymore. Sometimes sports can delay this process, allowing you to not have to face real life all at once, giving you a small feeling of invincibility that if you can make it to the pros, it'll make life easier.*

*Playing a sport can make you feel as if it will always be there for you when you stumble. It can allow you to feel like as long as you are doing well in that sport, everything else matters a little less. If your grades aren't that great, at least your sport can get you into college. If you're going through family or friend drama, at least you have cheering fans at your game or at your track meet. The same happens in dance, gymnastics, tennis, cheerleading,* soccer, football, and basketball. I think you get the picture.

I have been a part of sports since I was two years old. I've always loved every aspect of playing sports, the fellowship, competition, adrenaline, feeling in shape, and having teammates to share my accomplishments with and to support me in my failures. My athletic ability has been a part of me my entire life, a constant that I've felt I could always rely on. But one day, sports will fail me. One day I could have a horrible injury, or get in an accident, or get to the age where sports will not be an option for me anymore. This is why my identity cannot be in my athletic ability. Growing up is all about finding myself, finding out what I'm passionate about, and what kind of person I am outside of sports. How will I act when there's no longer a parent, teacher, or coach telling me every day what to do, or what I should, could, or will be one day?

The hardest part for me is realizing that I am not alone. Everyone is going through the exact same thing in their own way, and there are people who will support you and fight for you if you let them. Soon we will all have to leave high school, college, and sports behind, and we have to be ready for what real life will bring.

It's the oldest story in the world. One day you're seventeen and planning for someday. And then quietly and without you ever really noticing, that someday is today. And that someday is yesterday. And this is your life.

Learning how to balance your life and all its aspects can be a scary thing for a teenager. Without the proper guidance, it can feel like it's impossible. I couldn't get through tough times if I didn't have my parents and trusted friends by my side, fighting for me when I couldn't or didn't have the strength to fight for myself. As a former professional athlete, my dad knows what it is like to move beyond playing a sport on all levels, so it is comforting to know that I have someone who has transitioned from playing a sport. Let this book inspire you to experience life to the fullest after sports and guide you down the correct path for future success.

How could I not be so proud of the young lady that my daughter has become? In Lindsey's transition into college, it's important for her to know that I value her more than what she does and more than who she will become. I have always tried to balance my conversation between her academics and sports. There needs to be true accountability around both, so don't stop pushing your children (or yourself) to step up in all areas. We have to continue empowering our kids.

## Journal

Do you feel like you have enough responsibilities? If so, in what areas? If not: why?

_____

_____

_____

What is the one thing that scares you about the future?

_____

_____

_____

What's the most important thing in your life right now, and why do you give it that title? (When you find out the most important things in your life, you'll find out whether you're centered or not.)

_____

_____

_____

How do you perceive yourself? If you had to explain yourself to someone, what would you say?

_____

_____

_____

_____

## PART TWO:

## MAKING YOUR TRANSITION OUT OF THE LOCKER ROOM

The head coach of a team for the United Football League, which ran for a few years serving as a kind of minor league for football players and fans, called a meeting before final cuts were made on his team. He told all the players to be at this meeting on time. He warned, "If you're not on time, I'm going to cut you."

A friend who was there afterward reported, "I walked into the facility, and out came a player with tears in his eyes. And here comes Coach, following, shaking his head. 'He was late, and he got cut.' He wanted to make sure the players knew that his policies needed to be adhered to and taken seriously, and he admitted that it was 'really hard to do.' The player looked shell-shocked. He said, 'I have nothing. I have nowhere to go. I *don't know how to do anything else.*'"

The worst feeling as a human being is when you think that you don't have anything left to give in this world. But it's wrong. No one is blessed with just one gift; we are all given multiple talents. We can't always expect others to show or tell us what they are or how to use them, but we need to be aware that they exist.

Even though playing sports was hard, for many of us it was something we'd been doing since we were little kids. We were trained to perform, and it was both ingrained in our muscle memories and seared in our brains.

But when you quit playing a game you love, you have to train *new* muscles to learn the skills needed to create a life outside of the game. After all, football, basketball, car racing, baseball, tennis, golf: they're *games*. You need a *career*.

As people begin to search for something new to do, they might look for a role that's equal to the excitement of playing sports. But that's an easy way to be let down. Playing college or professional sports is a childhood fantasy lived out, sometimes coming with a fantasy salary that is hard to replicate outside of that life. Non-transitioned players (former players who keep thinking with the mindset of a current player) always have the wrong focus that does not allow them to see a better future; it keeps them in the past. Or they look for easy money—but if it sounds too easy, it probably is a trap or a con.

Players who haven't transitioned have not read the writing on the wall. As in Spencer Johnson's book *Who Moved My Cheese?* (a parable about people and change), people can keep going back to the wrong corridor, looking for where the cheese used to be. But it's in a whole new place now. That place requires structure, planning, sustainability, boundaries, and adapting to a different mindset of what is risk and what is reward.

The reality of having to adapt to a new mindset, indeed a new life, can sometimes be overwhelming at times. Transitioning from any aspect of life to another phase is demanding, even when every step is carefully planned. Regardless of how meticulously we prepare, sometimes we find ourselves moving in a direction that was not mapped out and doesn't feel right.

As you prepare or are in the midst of transitioning from one part of your life to the next, it's important to get to know yourself all over again: who are you *outside* of sports? Figuring that out may take you to some very dark places, but finding your own balance of confidence and humility can help you find your way back into the light.

# Chapter Four:

# YOUR TRANSPARENT LIFE ASSESSMENT

My dear friends and colleagues at game on Nation (www.gameonnation.com), Blair Bloomston and Steve Shenbaum, were kind enough to share some of their insight and curriculum to help improve your personal awareness, self-perception, and overall communication skills.

game on's program utilizes the science of game dynamics in a groundbreaking training technique called MILE, which embeds Mystery, Incentive, Laughter, and Empowerment to motivate clients to improve. Since 1997, their team of expert instructors (myself among them) has used game on's interactive curriculum to help build communication confidence for work and life, impacting some of the world's most elite teams and organizations. Some of their clients include NASCAR, Pittsburgh Pirates, Dallas Mavericks, LA Lakers, NFL Players Association, Florida State Football, United States Olympic Committee, Honda, and the USO. This program has also helped nine #1 overall NFL, NHL, and NBA draft picks prepare for the toughest career transition process of their lives, including Alex Smith, Sidney Crosby, Eli Manning, and Yao Ming.

On the following page, Blair and Steve explain in detail the value of one of their most popular self-awareness and self-confidence exercises: Coins.

## COINS

*by Steve Shenbaum and Blair Bloomston*

### Figuring Out Your Values

As children, we were often asked, "What do you want to be when you grow up?" and the answers were always positively and optimistically ambitious: president, firefighter, astronaut, rock star, superhero, professional athlete, etc. But be honest: when was the last time you woke up as an adult, looked in the mirror, and asked yourself *What do I want to be when I grow up? Who am I?* or *What makes me great?*

Your answer is probably NEVER.

As an athlete, whether you played professionally, in college, or as a weekend warrior, you achieved one of the most awesome and popular childhood dreams. You pushed your body and your mind to the peak of performance to rise to the top, while playing a game that you truly loved. But now you must prepare for a transition that makes your role as an athlete less of the main focus in your life. So how do you get back to the simplicity of *What do I want to be when I grow up?* when you're also faced with questions like *How do I pay my bills?, What skills do I have?,* and *I have no idea what I'm going to do next!*

To find the answer, we must exercise those muscles, just like you did when you were mastering your sport. You must build that communication and self-awareness muscle and practice to get stronger at these skills as you prepare for your career transition. Sprinters rely on exercises for speed, distance runners rely on exercises for endurance, and we rely on an exercise called Coins.

Over the next few pages, we'll explain how the game of Coins can help you feel prepared for your transition. The goal is to give you a new way of thinking about yourself. By figuring out some of your Coins, you can start to answer some of those pressing questions, like: *Who am I?* and *What are my strengths outside of sport?* As you build up your list of Coins by following along below, you'll be building a clearer understanding of how to understand your value and prove it to others.

Another purpose of Coins is to help you make strong, authentic connections anywhere there is a networking opportunity. You'll learn skills to help you stay calm and relaxed if you're nervous when talking to new people (as most of us are). You'll also discover the types of conversations that light you up and make you smile, helping you show the right amount of enthusiasm without seeming like you're trying too hard, or getting stuck in game-face mode. Playing the game of Coins will give you a clear plan for the types of things you should talk about in a networking conversation or when you've finally landed a job interview (*Hint:* people will want to know more about you than just your accomplishments as an athlete).

So now let's get to it...ready...set...game on!

### What Are Coins?

Coins are things that you value, and they also help define your *values.* They are hobbies, interests, activities, achievements, goals, and things that you have experienced in your life, things that light you up and make you smile when you think about them. Knowing your Coins helps you identify and understand your worth, both professionally and personally. They are an inherent and endless source for self-confidence, and gathering your Coins helps you quantify your value (similar to the way money has value). More importantly, knowing your Coins can help you define your values, i.e. your beliefs, principles, and moral code. Understanding your values comes from taking stock of the things that interest you, and recognizing whether these things have the potential to be destructive or harmful, or if they are positive, healthy influences in your life.

To play Round 1, take a second and try to think of at least three Coins that mean something to you, and that hopefully bring a smile to your face when you think about them.

Initially, many of the first Coins you might think of probably are related to your life as an athlete. For the majority of our clients, the thing they spend the most time doing usually dominates their first three Coins. So for our executive clients, their initial Coins are often work-related. For military personnel, many of their first Coins relate to their service. And we have found with our collegiate and professional athletes, when asked to think of their Coins, their primary focus is on sport. As you prepare to transition beyond your athletic career, we recognize that you've likely had many impressive athletic achievements. Your sports Coins probably start when you were an impressionable young dreamer, maybe as young as you can remember. An example of your sports Coins could be playing hide-and-seek with your neighborhood friends, or playing Pop Warner Football in elementary school. It could be the first time you won a race or earned a medal, or maybe it was college and the first time you set foot on campus. All of these amazing Coins that you have earned during your time as an athlete won't go away just because you are retiring or transitioning into a new career phase. That said, we need to take a quick moment right now to gather your Sports Coins and set them aside, giving you the chance to figure out some other areas of your life that have tremendous value.

If Round 1 was identifying and gathering your Sports Coins, Round 2 will be identifying and gathering your interests outside of your sport. So let's play Round 2. This time, grab a piece of paper and a pen, then find a stopwatch or your phone and set the timer to one minute. You now have 60 seconds on the clock to write down as many non-sports related Coins as you can think of. And . . . Go!

Now take a look at your list. Whether you wrote down 5 or 15 Coins during this one-minute drill, the point is that you are beginning to remember the many things that give you value, make you smile and light you up in your life outside of sport. The extreme demands of being a dedicated athlete can cause many Coins to end up on the back burner or be forgotten altogether. We spend so much time thinking about *WHAT* we have to do that we sometimes forget *WHY* we chose to do it. So if you struggled in trying to write down things outside of sport that bring a smile to your face, you are not alone. This is your chance to uncover some of the amazing things about your life that you haven't thought about in a while, to fuel you and prepare you for this next phase of your career.

*Universal Coins*

Round 3 of the game of Coins is about recognizing the areas in your life that have value, and that you can use to connect with others in networking situations and job interviews.

There are five "Universal Coin Categories" that nearly everyone in the world has in common. As you read through these categories, please keep your pen and paper handy, and write down any new Coins that you remember. You are now becoming a collector of your own value and values. The goal is for you to write down as many Coins as you can, focusing on those that have true, authentic meaning to you. Remember, you should avoid forcing it or trying to be someone you are not. For example, you shouldn't add "Speaks Spanish" to your resume if the only words you know are *hola* and *adios*. That's just setting yourself up for an awkward conversation...potentially in Spanish! Instead, try to focus on Coins that you already have, that are true and meaningful to you. We promise, the value you already have is enough; you just have to uncover it.

One last note before we launch into Round 3: your Coins should always be positive and appropriate. Let's be really clear here: positive coins are happy and uplifting, things that generally make everyone in the room feel good. It does not count as a positive if the happiness comes at someone else's expense or embarrassment, like the time your friend tripped and fell in the cafeteria and it was so hilarious to you. We call that laughing *at* (bad), rather than laughing *with* (good), and we want you to share stories that laugh with. Keeping your Coins appropriate is even more important, and to achieve this you need to focus on making everyone around you feel comfortable and to avoid "crossing the line." Since each person's line will be different based on their age, gender, beliefs, and life experience, a good rule of thumb is to avoid the "Sex, Drugs, and Rock & Roll" topics. Instead, try to think about topics that bring a smile to your face that would also be safe to share in front of your grandma, in front of your kids, or in a national press conference.

### Family Coins

When we think about things that we value, one of the first things that comes to mind is family. On your initial list of Coins you may have written down your children, your significant other, your parents, or brothers and sisters. Family is so powerful because these are people who have given you support through every stage of your athletic career until now, and they can be the best line of defense to keep you motivated, inspired, and supported going forward. When you think about your Family Coins, we want to challenge you to go deeper than just a simple list. Look back at the family members you may have already written down. Did you include their names? Is there a story that instantly comes to mind when you think of this person? For example, you may have written down "brother." It's more powerful for you to say you have a brother named Dave, who's a firefighter in Los Angeles. And it's even more powerful to say all that, and then have an extra story in your pocket about the time you and Dave took a road trip to Chicago for the first time and watched the Bears play at Soldier Field.

You might not share every detail about your Coin out loud, but it's important that you take some extra time to go deeper with each one. Take stock of the family members (friends can be included in this too) who have had your back. Get used to saying their names when you talk about them. Have an extra story in your pocket about a time that the two of you spent together that was incredibly exciting or special. In other words, love the details.

### Pet Coins

Another powerful topic to think about when gathering your Coins is pets. Our pets make a huge positive impact in our lives and we have found that pets cut through all socio-economic barriers. In fact, I'm willing to bet that you might have a picture of your pet on your phone or in your wallet right now. And if you do, go ahead take a second and look at that picture. Stop smiling right now! Gotcha.

For all the dog owners reading this, think about coming home from a long day, opening your front door, and seeing your dog there to greet you. Picture the tail wagging, tongue lolling, jumping up and down, excited just because you have come home. That's love, and it's unconditional. And if you don't have a dog, take a second to picture the special bond you have with your cat, snake, turtle, hamster, or fish. Our pets are our family too, and remembering to value them as Coins will absolutely help to light you up. Think about walking into a job interview, and knowing that you need to smile, and then using a quick memory of your current or childhood pet to get you there. You don't even have to talk about your pet, you just have to think about them, and you can't help but feel good. More importantly, your interviewer won't know why you're smiling; they'll just see you look confident.

Just like your family Coins, be sure to go further and think about stories and special quirks that your pets have. And try to always include the name of your pet when you think about them or talk about them. The name that you've chosen to give your pet can also reveal some really cool stuff about you. For example, knowing that you have a golden retriever named Luke Skywalker and a black lab named Darth Vader shows that you have an incredible sense of humor (and perhaps a passion for certain movies).

### Travel Coins

The next common Coin category is travel, and travel is excellent because you don't even have to have visited the place yet. Some of the best travel Coins are simply sharing places that you would love to see someday. When you think about your travel Coins, stay focused on the positive. It can be very tempting to share your airport horror stories, and we can all commiserate with bad travel experiences. But talking about negative things is not the way to play the game of Coins. Those non-positive memories might make you seem angry, and even if the conversation is flowing easily as you rant about your misery, that's not the kind of information you want others to remember about you. Use your travel Coins to keep the conversation moving in a positive direction. Your interviewer would love to know about the time you visited New York City, or traveled down the

Mississippi River, or scaled the Kilauea volcano in Hawaii.

### Food Coins

Food is another excellent Coin area, and this one is truly universal. On very rare occasions you might meet someone who has no interest in pets, has never traveled anywhere, and is an only child. The good news: they still have to eat. When you think about foods that you love, think also about restaurants that you enjoy, meals you know how to cook, and especially holiday traditions and special recipes that have meaning to your family. Talking about your food Coins is not the time to share your special dietary restrictions, to explain the benefits of a gluten-free lifestyle, or to express your addiction to all things sugary. Again, we want to keep these topics positive and universal, giving you the best chance to find things in common with others. Anytime you can combine a Food Coin with a Family Coin, and talk about holiday foods or recipes that you made with your grandparents, you get double bonus points. There is an amazing value to foods we eat when we are joined together in celebration, and talking about these experiences is powerful. Share these food stories, and collect them from others. You might even get a delicious, home-cooked meal out of it.

### Adventure Coins

The final universal category that nearly everyone has in common is what we call Adventure. Adventure includes fishing, hiking, running, hunting, skiing, scuba diving, skydiving, horseback riding, sailing, swimming, rollercoaster riding, snowboarding, treasure hunting, tight rope walking, and any other amazing, adrenaline-filled activity that you enjoy. In fact, a great example of an Adventure Coin could simply be teaching your kid to ride a bike, playing hide-and-seek, or playing catch. These activities can be adventures in and of themselves, and seem just as daunting as climbing Mount Kilimanjaro. As an athlete, you know the value of staying physically active and engaged, and your Adventure Coins are an important way for you to stay fit and stay moving. These are not only excellent topics of conversation, they might be new activities and interests that you should absolutely cultivate with your family and friends as you prepare for your career transition.

### Using Your Coins in Life

There are limitless areas in which to find Coins, and the five universal categories above are just a simple way to get you started. You'll also have many Coins that come from movies, music, TV shows that you watch, and other everyday activities that make you happy. And of course, at this point, you should go ahead and add back in all of the amazing and powerful Sports Coins that we asked you to set aside earlier. Your experiences as an athlete will actually be the number one thing that you are asked about during your transition, and you've probably already having these conversations on a daily basis. That said, we want you to expand your conversation comfort zone and to use ALL your Coins. When you're trying to find common ground with others, music, movies, and TV shows are extremely easy topics to start with. We encourage you to go beyond the usual, and whenever possible, try to incorporate new Coins into the conversation, especially things that would surprise the other person and give them a more accurate and thorough picture of you as a person.

### The Three Tie-Backs

Now that you've played your initial game of Coins, we encourage you to make it applicable to your life immediately. You don't have to keep a written list every time, but you should start to see each conversation as an opportunity to add new Coins into your bank. There are three "Tie-Backs" to Coins, that is, three concrete things for you to remember to help you use this game in life.

The first Tie-Back is "A Genuine Smile is Money." This tie-back reminds you to take stock of your Coins and have a thorough list of all the things that light you up, give you value, and bring a genuine smile to your face. You've already started this process by writing down your actual list. Once you have your list, carry it with you into every interaction. Some people choose to do this literally, and physically keep a copy of their Coins list in their wallet to look over quickly before they walk into the interview or networking situation. You can also bring your Coins with you metaphorically, and simply remember and think about one or two of them to help bring a smile to your face before you start the conversation.

The Second Tie-Back is "Be a Coin Collector." We've just spent a lot of time working on your Coins, and now you must set your list aside and try to collect other people's Coins. Being a collector takes so much of the pressure off of you in a conversation. You get to focus on the other person, and try to gather valuable Coins from them. As you do this, it's important to remember that you want to collect the Coins in a natural way. That is, you don't want to just rattle off question after question, and make the conversation feel more like an interrogation. If you see a natural opportunity to ask somebody about travel, or food, or their pets, do your best to weave in a question, but don't force it. Sometimes letting the conversation move on will actually give you an even better opportunity to collect a Coin in the future.

You'll also want to try to gather Coins that are very positive. We've all heard the cliché advice on how to ace a networking conversation: "Just get them to talk about themselves. People love to talk about themselves." But if you've ever been on the receiving end of this advice and had people asking you boring, inappropriate, or confrontational questions, you know that talking about yourself is the last thing you want to do in that situation. Getting people to simply talk about themselves is bad advice UNLESS you are able to get them to talk about things that they love. If you can move the conversation toward their Coins and topics of conversation that light them up, not only will the other person feel very comfortable talking, but they will walk away remembering how great they felt because of the conversation they just had with you.

The third Tie-Back is "Don't Underestimate Your Value." The more you gather your Coins, the more you'll realize that interests and achievements you've been taking for granted could actually be very interesting and valuable to the person you're talking to. In fact, it is sometimes the most simple, everyday, obvious Coins that we tend to forget that can make the most positive, authentic connections. A few good examples of undervalued Coins include loving In-N-Out Burger, being a former Boy Scout, or speaking more than one language. You will feel the impact of Tie-Back number three after achieving Tie-Backs one and two, when the conversation leads you to naturally discover Coins that you have in common with others. Shared Coins, even those that are just similar, create instantaneous bonds and trust between you and others. When two people find out that they are both older brothers, or that they have both been to Costa Rica, or that they stayed in the same dorm freshman year at their university, the conversation suddenly escalates to a new level of success. When Common Coins are discovered, both people not only care more about what the other person is saying, they will remember the conversation long after the interaction is through. Building common bonds and trust is the strongest impact of Coins. Uncovering the many athletic and non-athletic talents, achievements, hobbies, and interests that you can use to connect with others is the key to feeling truly confident and never again underestimating your value. To increase your chances of finding Common Coins during your upcoming networking opportunities and during job interviews, make sure to always keep your list of Coins with you (Step One) and do your best to think less about yourself and more about the other person as you collect their Coins (Step Two).

### It's All About You

Creating a transparent life assessment starts with you. We can't achieve growth in this area by just telling one another to improve. Even most well-meaning advice from our supportive friends and family—statements like *Be confident, Be yourself, Just relax,* or *You've got this*—are just words at the end of the day, and run the risk of sliding in one ear and out the other. Showing each other images and videos to inspire improvement is slightly better, but it can also be ineffective, and even a little ridiculous. For example, at some point in your athletic career, you may have seen a motivational poster on the wall in a locker room or training room. While the great blue whale breaching out of the Arctic Ocean with the words *Believe in Yourself* is a nice image, it's certainly not a game-changer. We have never had a client win a championship and when asked, "What inspired you to win?" respond by saying "It was the Whale poster. I looked at it right before I took the field."

You deserve more than statements and pictures, and practicing Coins as an exercise is a solution on HOW to improve. Playing this game gives you the chance to actively exercise your communication muscles so you can meta-phorically and literally move yourself to improve. With Coins, you now have a simple, tangible way to answer the questions *Who am I?* and *What makes me great?* Not only can you gather this information for yourself, you have the puzzle pieces to share your story in a networking conver-sation and authentically prove your value. This is why the Coins exercise is imperative to your personal growth. Just like the speed exercise improves the sprinter and the endur-ance exercise improves the long distance runner, collecting your Coins is the exercise that will help you improve as a person. This is your new sport. This is your new goal. If you approach it with the same commitment to excellence, discipline, and activation that made you such a successful athlete, this new journey will be one filled with value and *values*. And you will be rich with transparency.

I love how playing the game Coins helps me to remember what I value in my life. Some of my coins are my faith; watching a movie with peanut M&M's, popcorn, and a slushy on my birthday (or any movie day); watching my daughter Lindsey run track; remem-bering how my mom worked for so many years while taking care of us kids every day without complaining (not in front of us, anyway).

**Journal:**

What are your coins?

_____

_____

_____

_____

_____

_____

Coins sometimes change. Over the past two years, what has changed in your life that now holds more value to you?

_____

_____

_____

_____

_____

_____

How does it feel when people value you and share that with you?

_____

_____

_____

_____

_____

_____

How important is it that you share how you value others?

_____

_____

_____

_____

_____

_____

## Chapter Five:

## THE BLACK HOLE: WORKING THROUGH GRIEF

*Immediately after I retired, at the advice of family and close friends, I took about a year to try to figure out what I wanted to do next. Although I had originally thought I might want to go into law, my interests had changed and I was unsure about embarking on that new route at my age (38). I had some fears in terms of what I wanted to do. With the realization that I was no longer going to be playing football, I became depressed. I felt this way because for the first time in my life, I was not doing something that I loved to do. A professional football player is exactly what I wanted to be when I grew up, and I had already achieved that, and had achieved it at an early age in life. After that ended, the feeling was like, now what? That was a little hard to deal with.*

*—Hardy Nickerson*

When I first transitioned out of the NFL, I thought, *What in the world just happened to me?* For years, I had known that an end to me playing football could happen at any time, but it still came abruptly for everyone in my house and was a shock emotionally.

On paper, I had all the tools that I needed for success: I was educated, had an entrepreneurial spirit, was highly motivated, had my family's and friends' support, and had a great resource pool along with a strong faith.

But I felt paralyzed.

Fear and doubt weighed me down to such an extent that I

couldn't make a move. While in the NFL, I had a clear-cut path of what I needed to do to stay employed, but out in the real world, I didn't know what my next step should be.

When you're let go (cut) from a team, or injured out, you keep up a façade that things are going just great. But things were not all right for me. I had many dark nights in my soul, questioning my abilities, questioning my resourcefulness, questioning whether I could provide for my family, questioning everything I'd ever done.

As a result, I made some bad moves. One was opening up a restaurant. I thought I had been smart about it: I met with Carolina Panthers owner Jerry Richardson after I retired from playing, and we discussed business (he's a former NFL football player and very successful owner of the Bojangles' franchise). I formed a partnership called Team8s with my former teammate Doug Evans. There was an investor group, and we had meetings with bankers, lawyers, NASCAR people. Everybody was just nodding their heads at what the bankers were telling us, so excited that the money would soon start rolling in.

But my friend Jeff Mandel asked all the tough questions—he's as sharp as a tack. He crosses his t's and dots all his i's. He was confident and knew how to ask the right questions. I used to think, *Why does he have so many questions and others don't?* He just felt something. Even though people listened to him, no one wanted to sound the alarm. Something was wrong and nobody wanted to hear it. They disregarded it.

The restaurant was a New Orleans / low-country type of restaurant, set on a great piece of lakeside property outside of Charlotte, where people could moor their boats as well as come by car. But I had nagging regrets as everything came together for the opening: I had always thought that the place would be better as a sports bar, since the investor group was sports people, and because of the casual setting. But then on the opposite side of the spectrum, I had nightmares about somebody driving home drunk and getting killed and killing others from the alcohol they drank at my restaurant bar.

I realized later that I hadn't really spent any time praying about the decision to open the restaurant. I went into it without any soulful reflection, and those nightmares and nagging feelings were a sure sign of my mixed feelings about this business.

One night at the restaurant, I had asked a group of friends join me at dinner. We were sitting around the table having a great time; I was feeling like a big-shot entertaining my friends at my own restaurant. Just then, the door opened and a couple of sheriffs came in. One of the managers came over to me and whispered, "They're getting ready to shut down the restaurant." I was mortified. How was I going to get my friends out of the restaurant before this whole scene went down? What would I say?

The sight of those two sheriffs, putting on their hats and adjusting them just so before they walked farther into the restaurant is one I'll never forget. I had absolutely no idea why the sheriffs had come to shut us down and I was horrified. One of the people I had invited was my mentor. I think I managed to get my friends out before they saw the restaurant being shut down.

I later found out that the people our group had hired to manage the restaurant weren't paying taxes on any of the income we received. The sad thing is that the restaurant had so much promise and the potential to do well. I lost over $38,000. So much for that money pouring in.

I wasted so much time to trying to make up that money. I became obsessed with it, and it sent me down into a dark place. I joined a multilevel marketing group, trying to find a way to replace that money, fast. But it didn't make me feel good—I wasn't creating anything. I felt stuck, used, stifled, alone, and just not in a good place.

I didn't know it immediately, but eventually I recognized: I was in a black hole.

## What is a Black Hole?

The Black Hole is a real phenomenon in the universe. It's a place in space where gravity pulls so forcefully that even a beam of light cannot get out (it's called "black" because it has absorbed all of the light). Since light cannot get out, a black hole cannot be seen on the inside. However, just as what goes up must come down, as a black hole sucks objects in, it also spits them out.

Most people think that black holes are enormous vacuums that destroy everything in their pathway; however this isn't exactly how the physics of a black hole works. In a black hole, you can't see over the edge, so you can't forecast or predict what's going to happen inside. Only a small amount of matter actually falls into the black hole itself, while the remaining matter circles and circles, swirling in space, unable to escape the relentless gravitational pull.

You can find yourself in your own black hole because of grief. You *miss* the life you used to have. This is a desolate and lonely place to be. It feels like no one understands where you are, and you're too scared to tell anyone the truth. People will ask, "How can I help?" But you don't really know the answer, because you've never felt so surrounded by a dark place before.

Outside is dark, and inside you feel abandoned. Your phone has stopped ringing. You stop getting invited to gatherings. It feels like your former teammates are thinking, *What do you really have to offer me/us anymore?* You question your worth to them—to anyone.

You might also be in the black hole grieving over what you have squandered. You had such a great opportunity, and you didn't enjoy it like you should have. You bought gifts instead of investing the way you knew you should have. You didn't seize the day, and it flew by; you thought you had at least one more year to make it right. You wish you could do it all over again—maybe it would last longer. You start saying, "If I knew what I know now, then…"

Sometimes landing in the black hole comes because of an inevitable transition, and sometimes something shocking happened. Sometimes you just made a decision that went wrong.

We can feel like we're in a black hole over lost careers, failed relationships, parenting issues, a death in the family, and illness. We miss what we had, and we want it back, but we know it's not possible. Your ex-wife is remarried. Your kids who you wanted to spend more time with are grown and busy with their own lives. Your shoulder is so busted you can never throw again. Your high school football career is over and now it's time to grow up. The manufacturing industry in your town has closed down and moved, and there are no more jobs left in your hometown. Your knees are too arthritic to run again, and you miss that feeling of physical wellness that comes from being able to run down the street without pain.

Many men and women have been to this place and found themselves unable to get out; their lights are forever dimmed. This is truly tragic: we all make mistakes, we all have bad things happen to us, but to be successful in life you must be resilient. Grief and depression are a natural part of life, but the important thing is not to stay stuck.

When you are in the black hole, it can make you really angry, anxious, or nervous. Those emotions start filling your head and you might do things that are out of character for you, or you don't process conversations correctly, and people don't recognize your actions as being typically yours. Somebody may try to intervene to calm you down, and alleviate that stress, anxiety, nervousness, and anger, but the longer you have been in that state, the harder it's going to be to get out of it—but it's not impossible.

Heisman Trophy winner Eddie George, who retired from football after nine seasons as a professional, said about his transition, "There was a point in time where I would wake up and just say, 'OK, what should I do today?'...For a long time, having this unfocused thought led to unfocused behaviors." George suffered from depression, chased women, and never felt that instant "high" he'd felt when winning a game on Sunday.

Though the science of black holes is complicated, there are parallel lessons that apply to life situations. In space, quantum physics leaves a trail of information, and in our lives our behavior leaves a trail that mirrors our emotional decisions. Decisions lead our actions and create cause-and-effect as we set the behavior into motion.

## Fear

When you are stuck in a black hole, one of the reasons you're stuck is fear.

Fear is a conditioned response that occurs from preconditioned stimuli. On the surface, you might describe fear as the response to perceived danger. Three things occur universally in a fear reaction: the experience of apprehension or anxiety, the associated physiological response, and the emotional response. Fear is neither explicitly good nor bad; it can be both.

It's important to recognize that a lot of times the black hole is an *illusion*, because it's triggered by fear, and doubt in yourself and your choices makes it real.

Troy Vincent, fifteen-year NFL player and current senior vice president for NFL football operations, says:

> The one piece of advice I would give to anyone in transition is that "there is nothing to fear but fear itself." I had learned at a very early age through my pastor that the acronym for fear was: False Evidence Appearing Real. It's not real, but it's the illusion that something is about to happen, and you fix your mind on that to say "Oh, this can't work." I say, "No! It's like a shadow. It's not real. It's the false evidence of something being real." Fear is what holds people back, and is bondage in itself.
>
> I would recommend to everyone not to allow fear to keep you from moving forward, as it does for so many millions of people who fear failure. Failure is good sometimes. Don't be afraid to fail.

By asking real questions to the people around you, you can determine whether what you're feeling is really a crisis, or FEAR, as Troy put it. Is this really happening because of someone else, or are you responsible? Why is it stopping you from doing what you want to do? How does one answer these relevant questions? You must first admit that you are in this place of FEAR.

## Getting Out

If you find yourself in a black hole, how do you get out of it?

There is no one formula for getting out, and no specific timeline. Identifying a formula that will work for you can be a process, and will probably involve a lot of trial and error.

I've had failures, and beat myself up about them. I had so much information coming at me from my friends, books that I was reading, and courses that I was taking, that I had to ask the questions: *What fits into my life? What does this mean? And what should I do?*

You keep searching and seeking for something that's going to bring you the same feelings of value and worth as what you've left behind, that big golden ticket. You have to take the same energy and motivation and channel it to something new—and something new isn't always bad. Companies love to hire athletes for various reasons, but one obvious reason is because we have a proven innate work ethic that is priceless.

Every human being experiences a time of grieving over something that's lost, or guilt at having made a bad decision that's led them to a bad place. While grief, like transition, is a natural part of life, how you recover and gain wisdom to get out of the black hole is valuable to everything you do going forward.

Black holes occur in a set of certain conditions, just like our problems. A black hole is formed when a massive star collapses at the end of its life cycle, and can continue to grow as it collects debris into its gravitational pull.

For me, the solution rested on reconnecting with my faith. I had to gird myself into the Word. I had to re-create my relationship with the Lord. I couldn't depend on people and processes more than the foundation of my faith. My mom always used to say, "Fight your battles on your knees." Fighting is not going to be with my arms or my hands; it's going to be with my faith—that's the most consistent way. And when you're finished praying, get up and take action.

*But someone will say, "You have faith, and I have works." Show me your faith without your works, and I will show you my faith by my works. You believe that there is one God. You do well. Even the demons believe—and tremble! But do you want to know, O foolish man, that faith without works is dead?*
*—James 2: 18-20*

You didn't just happen to fall into the black hole. You need to own that you are responsible for being there. How do you accept the responsibility for being in a place when you have no idea how you arrived? I don't know what your faith is and I'm not going to assume that it's the same as mine, but I know that the Holy Spirit allows me to discern every direction and every destination in my life. What is your process for reasoning? What is your faith? What or who do you have faith in and how does it serve you right now where you are?

I speak with athletes who have been stuck in the same hovering pattern for years, some as long as decades, trying to find their place in the world, trying to find their significance, seeking value, trying to locate their purpose. This book is not about judgment, but about finding transparency of one's self, self-awareness, accountability, assistance in helping us understand that we can't do life alone. In the Bible, God always talks about sending two, so that one can serve as a witness and that both can sharpen each other.

The book of Exodus in the Bible tells a story about Moses and how God allowed him to go into a desolate place. This place was one of darkness, confusion, and no direction. Moses's journey is relevant to anyone who is going through the transformation of finding their true destiny. Your journey is not going to be easy, and it will not exactly resemble anyone else's, but there are always lessons to be learned from the journeys of others. Even if you are not religious, I recommend that you read Exodus to see an example of what can happen when the mindset stays the same, but the destination changes. The results will still resemble the old. Don't get stuck in a bad place for twenty years because you keep waiting for someone to rescue you.

I go around the country telling current players that they need to prepare for no longer being players. The more preparation you do early, the better. Think of it as preventative medicine for your and your family's future emotional health. The more steps you take now to avoid going into the black hole, the easier your transition will be.

Once you do enter into the black hole, it's really difficult to get out, but not impossible. In Matthews 19:26 and Philippians 4:13, we are reminded not just that we can do all things, but that we are never alone while doing them. You will start to see that we are always transforming as we create more clarity as to where we are going.

## A Team Effort

You have to get yourself out of the black hole *for* yourself first, but you shouldn't try to do it *by* yourself. If you think this is a problem with a solo solution, you're going to stay there. Just as one person can't win a team game, one person cannot free themselves from a bleak situation.

You need family support, and by this I mean your chosen family as well: friends. This is not a time where we want yes-men or women in our lives, because they are not going to challenge us—they just might sympathize and say that we are doing the right thing by indulging in our grief. You need people who care about you and challenge you to get your butt out of bed, to get out of the hole. It helps to have somebody who has been down this road, and not someone who has never suffered disappointment or hardship. That's why our testimony of our past is so valuable. When you have recovered your self, please tell others your story, and don't underestimate the value of your voice.

No one wants to be stuck in a black hole, but it can be debilitating. You may feel like you can't do *anything* to get yourself unstuck. Your social support system needs to get help for you, to get the healing process started and hold you up as you go through it. NFL transition coaches were trained to assist players through this process; no matter what your past or future career path, counselors and therapists are trained to teach you how to get you back on your feet. Start researching the different resources that might be available to you or your family. When I blew out my knee playing for the Carolina Panthers in 1999, my wife, Chandra, had to cover for me in different areas until I recovered enough to operate at a certain capacity. Stop trying to figure out the solution alone and reach out to someone now. Some of the resources at the end of this book will assist you in this part of your transformation.

Sometimes you need a professional to help you: meeting with a psychologist, counselor, mentor, pastor, or life coach will really assist you in getting out of the denial phase and facing facts: *This is where you are. This is a terrible and heartbreaking situation to be in, but you can make your way out of it.* Use this professional as someone you can bounce ideas off, vent to, strategize with, and be fully transparent to. Ultimately the problem that needs solving is: Where you are going to go next?

> **TIME TO HEAL**
>
> Almost everyone in sports gets injured competing. Think of a time when you got injured, and the time spent recuperating from that injury—surgery, healing time, physical therapy. You spent a lot of time sitting on the sideline, watching the others play. At times, you probably didn't feel like you were a valuable part of the team. It's an isolating experience, and a good window into how it feels to no longer being able to play the game. Try to remember how you handled it emotionally. What did you do to make yourself feel better? What did you say to yourself? What did you do to stay connected to your teammates?

## Steer Yourself Away from Negative Thinking

The way we think impacts the way we feel and behave. But what comes first: the feeling or the negative thought? For instance, you might think: *I know I'm feeling terrible, but I'm also having a lot of negative thoughts.* Am I feeling terrible because I'm focusing on my negative thoughts? Dr. Will Mayer, a sports psychologist and psychology professor, has developed a system for his clients called STER (pronounced *steer*). You can impact your feelings by examining the way you're thinking.

Situation  Thought  Emotion  Reaction

If you do not like your reaction to a given situation, examine what's going on in this diagram. Let's say a student is taking an exam—so the *Situation* is the exam, the *Thought* is that she's not going to do well, the *Emotion* is anxiety, and the *Reaction* is she's going to run out of the exam room, freaking out.

The student cannot change her situation; she needs to take that test. She can identity that her emotion is *anxiety*, and her thought is *I am going to perform poorly*. It is fairly easy to see that the reaction in this situation was a direct product of her thought in her given situation. Knowing this, the student trained in STER has the awareness that in order to change her reaction, since she cannot change her situation, she must change her thought.

She can say to herself, "Yes, this is a big exam, and I need to change my reaction. I need to breathe deeply to calm my body down enough so that I can take the test. I need to focus. I need to think about what I want, not what I don't want."

How does this apply to your escape from the black hole?

If you can change the situation, do it. If your job is making you feel awful, get a new one. If you can not afford to leave your job, you have to negotiate with yourself as to why you need to stay and then establish a date for change to happen. If your time feels empty, fill it with something fulfilling. Go out and find a homeless shelter that needs volunteers; get involved with Big Brothers Big Sisters and serve. If you are overspending, downsize your budget.

But when you *can't* change the situation, you need to go to a more problem-solving operation. You need to focus on: *How do I help my emotional state by both changing the way I'm thinking and behaving? What do I want? What steps can I take to get closer to what I want? What skills do I have that will help me get there?*

The next time you see that your thoughts and behavior are negative, trace them back. What's really going on? What can you do to change that scenario? What was the cause?

### Changing Black Hole Behavior

A person who is depressed and in the black hole needs structure: Get out of bed. Set up a routine in your life. The worst thing is to have NOTHING to do. Walk around the block with your dog. Meet a friend for lunch. Go to the gym. Spend some time researching new jobs or careers. If you set up a schedule for every day, you don't have to worry or think about what you're going to do. You can focus your thought energy on your next steps. If you feel like you need some external motivation, look into working with a life coach or try signing up for a 10-minute coach at my10minutecoach.com.

Once you have some structure, build on your routine. Add new things; change things that aren't making you feel positive. And be sure you make some time each day to identify the negative feelings you have and acknowledge them. If you don't have awareness of what is holding you down, you can't push it off and move forward.

> *Structure is very important to me, and I think the NFL and how you function in it every day sets you up to expect that type of structure. I had become so used to the NFL's regimented way of life that it spilled over into my life after playing. I do better with schedule and routines, so I needed to have a set plan for my day, every day. I always try to set goals, and then I can measure how I am doing day-to-day, week-to-week, and yearly.*
>
> —Hardy Nickerson

## A Few Words About Denial

Dr. Myles Monroe said, "The most dangerous thing in life is for a person to have success." If we identify ourselves by our past success, we may spend the rest of our lives using it as a measuring tool, instead of viewing every opportunity as its own new set of challenges, with the full spectrum of possibility for success and failure.

There may be individuals out there who are still holding out hope that things are going to turn around. Maybe their ex will come back. Maybe the job they got laid off from will suddenly rehire. Maybe the general manager will call and say you're needed to come play again.

Those people are saying:

- "I haven't been given a fair chance."
- "They don't know how much this means to me."
- "I want to leave on *my* terms."
- "I'm going to spend the rest of my waking moments preparing to get back in."

Here's some of the language you might hear from a player who has not transitioned out of the life of a sport:

- "They never gave me an opportunity to show what I can really do."
- "I believe if I work really hard I can make a comeback." (This from a player who has been out of the league for 12 years, and he still thinks he's going to get the call to come back and play pro ball.)
- "I could have made it into the pros."
  "Oh, did you play in college?"
  "No, I played in high school. But I was better than the person who started, but the defensive coach didn't like me." (This

player didn't make it into college football, and he blames his high school coaches.)

- "I should have been a first-rounder, but I was a fifth-rounder because of a decision I made in college." (This person keeps rekindling the past, as if it's going to change the present.)

Compare the above conversations with the type of language you might hear from a player who has transitioned out of the mindset of playing a sport.

- "No, I don't miss the game. I'm so excited about the new opportunities that are going on in my life right now."
- "I miss the camaraderie of the locker room, but I've created so many new, great relationships and memories in my life now."
- "I miss the game, but I have so much more life in front of me"

If you truly feel like you'll spend the rest of your life regretting that you didn't make an effort to get back in the game, then pursue it with some real stipulations. You need some realistic assessment parameters before the pursuit begins. Put an actual deadline on the calendar for this dream. Declare it to those around you to make you accountable to sticking to it. There are rare exceptions where it's worked. Be self-aware and confident in yourself and the situation by being real with your chances. Without a deadline, you might realize that three years have passed, and you're the last person to see that your chances have evaporated with that dream, and think, *I hung on so long, I wish I had I gotten to this next stretch of my life earlier.*

Denial can occur when you haven't played out all your hopeful scenarios in the cold light of day. You've had a career-ending injury but somehow you think you'll play again. Really? Is that what the doctor says? The factory closed in your small town, and nobody is coming to take its place, but you still want to stay in your hometown where there are no jobs.

If you're in it that deep, you might need others to point it out to you. Sometimes denial can only be solved by the confrontation of others, who can tell it to you straight. Strong friends will tell you the truth even when they know you won't like it. Seek out those people if you can, and ask whether they think you're in denial.

One quarterback who found success didn't give up trying to get back into the NFL. Josh McCown comes from a football family: his younger brother is Luke McCown, a fellow NFL quarterback, and his older brother, Randy, was a quarterback for Texas A&M. Josh played for the Arizona Cardinals, the Detroit Lions, the Oakland Raiders, and the Miami Dolphins. In his last season with the NFL as a Carolina Panther, his job was to go out onto the field and kneel down to eat up time at the end of the quarter in two games, after back-up quarterback Matt Moore was injured. Then he got cut.

In 2010, Josh joined the Hartford Colonials, part of the newly formed United Football League. The tickets to UFL games were less expensive, so as to make the games more family friendly, and the players would be either veterans such as McCown, or younger players who never ended up getting drafted. McCown threw over 1,000 yards passing at the end of the league's first and only season.

In August 2011, McCown was signed to the 49ers, who then released him three weeks later. He then immediately started coaching high school football in a suburb of Charlotte, before being picked up by the Chicago Bears. He now is signed with the Tampa Bay Buccaneers for a $10-million, two-year contract.

This is the dream scenario for a player who still thinks he can be in the game, but note McCown's flexibility, and willingness to try new ventures, such as the UFL, and even high school coaching. He was never static; he was always moving.

### Resilience

Athletes are generally very resilient people. They've made a career out of getting knocked down and getting back up again, getting injured and healing, being the loser in the race only to train harder and become the winner. With structure and discipline, and the support of honest and encouraging people, finding your passion can be a whole lot easier.

Try not to let failures or setbacks place you on the road back to the black hole. My friend's mother-in-law was just scammed out of $5,000. She doesn't have $5,000. She can't let it go that she got scammed. When you can't let go of something bad that happened to you—a mistake you made, an unfair assumption about you, then you become your own victim. Nothing can replace it—you've got bitterness, anger, and resentment. You feel stupid and continually beat yourself up. We all make mistakes and must learn to forgive ourselves.

On the other hand, my friend Beth, a single parent who owns her own business, recently had a different reaction when her client refused to pay her $2,000 invoice. Rather than following the suggestions of her angry friends to take her client to court and send that client emails every day demanding to be paid, she simply moved on to her large list of waiting clients, and refused to dwell on the bad actions of one client. Very soon, she had made up that money and gained better clients.

You've got to let failures go. Whether it's a $10,000 loss or a $500 loss, it hurts to let it go. (Well, $10,000 is way harder to let go than 500 bucks, let's be real here.) But your well of knowledge will not run dry with ideas or creativity because of it. Your focus needs to be in the future. And look upon the lesson that you got from your loss as something of value—it shows you what not to do the next time. Beth knew she shouldn't have worked with that client, but she did anyway. My friend's mother-in-law knew that that deal sounded too good to be true, but she didn't listen to her inner voice and got scammed. And I didn't follow through on paying attention to the management of the restaurant I owned, instead taking a distant backseat on the day-to-day operations. I don't let that happen anymore.

But there will be those who refuse to leave the black hole. A friend of Dr. Mayer's calls him at least once a year, asking about whether there is anything more he can do for a friend of his who is clinically depressed. They ran down the list of everything that they've tried. "Ok, are you sure there's not anything more I can do?" Dr. Mayer told him, "You've tried everything. It's up to him to take the first step. Let's hope he does it, for not just his sake, but also for his family."

**Stop the Worry About Failure**

Tell me one thing in your life that you failed at doing by putting 100 percent of your focus, effort, and motivation into being successful. If you try something and it fails, how do you get back up and get into the game? Did you throw a touchdown pass your first time on the field? Sink the three-pointer every time you shot one? Hit a home run or base hit every time at bat? And besides, you can't live with without regret unless you know you tried. I remember the first time my daughter Lindsey tried to ride her bicycle without training wheels. The thought of falling and failing petrified her, and she wanted to quit plenty of times, but I knew that if she continued trying and succeeded, the success would drown out the failure and help her develop more confidence in other areas.

The fear of failure can be both debilitating and motivating.

Baseball players are used to seeing their failures posted as statistics. A successful player is one who has a batting average over .300, so for every ten balls thrown at them, they hit three. Baseball's minor leagues help groom players to either get used to the idea that their dream is going to come true and they're going to be called up to the big leagues, or that this is as good as it gets for them. Perhaps this is why baseball players cope with their transition better out of the sport than other types of sports players. They are used to the concept that life is all about failure, that even doing really well, you're only going to hit three balls out of ten.

Those who have been particularly successful in their chosen sport are often reluctant to be seen failing at any other part of their life. They have been viewed as blessed, gifted, a golden child, and they don't want to tarnish that image. But history has shown time and again that nobody is impervious to failure, whether in their personal lives or on the job. Failure shows that you were willing to take a risk and that you're human.

For instance, it's incredibly hard to get a book deal from a major publisher. Once you have written a book, you have to first get a literary agent to take you on, and then you have to hope that your agent finds the right editor who loves your project and wants to acquire the rights. The odds are very small. And yet, the number of successful authors who were turned down by agent after agent, publisher after publisher, is astonishing. Was the agent who picked J. K. Rowling out of a pile of unknown authors a genius, or just awake that day, or one who knew that he could take a risk? After that first *Harry Potter* book was turned down by twelve different publishers over the course of a year and then finally bought, its success was slow, but steady. Now, with an estimated net worth of over a billion dollars, thanks to book sales, the most successful film series in history, and a theme park at Universal Studios, J. K. Rowling is very happy that she didn't give up trying after a year of rejections.

**Journal:**

On a scale of 1-10, how do your emotions affect your decision-making process, as opposed to your rational thinking?

How does it make you feel to know that you're not alone?

Add positive words to HOPE below. Add positive connotations to each letter that are personal to you.

H _____
_____
_____
_____

O _____
_____
_____
_____

P _____
_____
_____
_____

E _____
_____
_____
_____

How does it make you feel when you make a breakthrough? Why do you think it's important to celebrate your breakthroughs? How should you celebrate your breakthroughs?

_____
_____
_____
_____

**Chapter Six:**

## LET THERE BE LIGHT—AND
## LET THE GAMES BEGIN!

*And God said, "Let there be Light"; and there was light. And
God saw that the light was good; and God separated the
light from the darkness. God called the light Day, and the
darkness he called Night.*

*...And God said, "Let there be lights in the vault of the sky
and separate the day from the night, and let them serve as
signs to mark sacred times, and days, and years."*
*—Genesis1:3–5, 14*

Getting out of the black hole and seeing a glimmer of light helps
you mark sacred times, days, and years, as it says in Genesis.
Darkness is inevitable, but so too is light.

*To everything there is a season, and a time to every purpose
under Heaven...a time to break down, and a time to build up.*
*Ecclesiastes 3:1–3.*

My great friend Troy Vincent, works every day with current, former,
and future athletes, to point them on the path to successful next
careers, talks openly about his own transitions, both within his athletic career and moving forward from there.

*I would say imagining life without sports is something that is very difficult for a teenager, let alone a collegiate or professional athlete. As a professional, I learned that the transition piece is constant in everyone's life—as a child, as an adolescent, as an adult. Transition is constantly taking place for not just the athlete, but also for siblings and parents. There is both physical transition and mental transition. So I was accustomed and very aware that transition is part of my life's journey.*

*I had been preparing for transition from the day I arrived in the NFL. The day that I was drafted by the Miami Dolphins back in 1992, I was told that the inevitable was going to happen. I knew that my body had an expiration date, so my process of transitioning took place daily, every off-season, from internships to job changes to working in a corporate office. That took place for fifteen years. So transition was constant throughout my athletic life cycle, and it still is today, in my daily life.*

*When it was time for me to leave the NFL, there was no fear, but there was a level of excitement. I was ready. My body had physically played itself out. And the anticipation of taking on the next challenge in my life was exciting. I took what I had learned from football, from my past experiences, and applied that to the rest of my life.*

*Setting realistic expectations is crucial. It's very important for those who are in transition, either from one profession to another, from trade school to college, college to the real world, whether it's a professional transition or a sports transition, to talk about setting realistic expectations. This is because many athletes don't have a lot of work experience, so they shouldn't set expectations that are unrealistic, such as "As soon as I finish, I'm going to walk into a Fortune 500 company and run it."*

*I had realistic expectations, the first of which was to make sure that I engaged with my family in a way that I had not over the past fifteen years as a player. Second was to make sure that I engaged my business partners by showing my commitment in the area of business, like how my wife and I had entered into and engaged with the team throughout my playing experience. Third, and very importantly, I knew what I was and what I wasn't, and I never tried to be something that I wasn't. Lastly, I acknowledge my shortcomings, which allows me—and it's still a work in progress—to continue to set realistic expectations for myself, my family, and my professional development.*

*Transition is constant because my family—my wife and five children—both throughout my playing experience and today, are transitioning as well. So it's very important that your wife and your children are included in your transition, that they are acknowledged as having the transition take place for them as well—for instance, going from sitting in the stands to watching on TV, and from being treated as VIPs to everyday people. The family also goes through transition, particularly my wife, but they embrace it and we acknowledge it all together.*

I love what Troy has to say, not only because I respect and admire him both as a man and a friend, but also because he mentions several points I want to address in this chapter to help you see the rays of light in your transition that will guide you to a whole new world.

## Transition Your Family and Friends

When I retired from the NFL in 2000, my wife Chandra wasn't used to me being home every second of the day. I abruptly threw a monkey wrench in her daily routine. We must remember that it's not just you who is going through a transition, but your family and friends. A lot of relationships get damaged as a result of a change in life. You have to be mindful—and they need to be mindful—that not only your life is changing, but theirs as well. The way in which you spend your time affects their time. If you used to be away traveling, you are likely to be at home more now. If you always received VIP treatment because of your status as a player, for a majority of players it will start fading away more and more. Your insecurity at your new role in life may trigger their insecurity.

Keep your friends' and family's feelings in your thoughts as you go through this time. Don't ignore them. Keep the lines of communication with them open, about what they're going through, and what you're going through. Spending time with them will help keep you grounded and remind you of what your values are.

> *Having a strong support group in place helped tremendously. The most valuable part of my team as I transitioned was my wife. She understood what I was going through and helped me sort through the things I had interest in doing while at the same time being supportive.*
>
> —Hardy Nickerson

### Set Realistic Expectations

As Troy said, set realistic expectations for yourself. You're not going to transition out of one place in life and expect to assume a leadership position in another place immediately. Just because you had status in one place doesn't mean that it translates. Be humble. Take slow but steady steps toward success. It is important to know what being realistic is to you and not what it means to everyone else. Being realistic will allow you to make sound decisions and listen to sound advice. It is not setting goals that are unattainable for you or for others to attain. We'll discuss this more in Part Three.

### Show Commitment

At the NFL, Troy and his team have revolutionized the professional and personal growth of players and their families by directing essential support programs and services such as The Legends Community, Professional Development, Benefits, Insurance, and Transitional Programs. Troy works closely with NFL executives, coaches, and players to ensure his department meets the evolving needs of players.

Troy is committed to helping current and former players, and his work shows that. Wherever you have passion, you need to show commitment to the cause.

Your commitment here is to having a successful transition. While that may involve weathering a few failures, the goal is to keep moving forward, thoughtfully. Being stuck in one place is not an option, even if you feel very comfortable and safe there. Commit to yourself, your family, and friends that you will find a new purpose, a new role, a new goal, and a new destination.

> *I took advantage of the programs that the NFL offers for players. It was part of doing my due diligence during my tenure in the NFL. I got involved in a broadcasting seminar offered by our team (Panthers), and put money away through the NFL 401(k) program and other annuity options. I got counsel from other players whom I respected and who had already transitioned into "normal" life. Mike Haynes, long time corner for the Patriots and the Raiders, told me about radio and TV in 1992, and I pursued those media while playing football. I wanted to give myself some viable options. I graduated with a BA in computer science and was willing to tap into that resource as well. I am truly blessed.*
> —*Eugene Robinson*

## Be Authentic

When you play sports, you are often told to put on a "game face." You get in the zone and try to psych out the other players around you with your focus, grit, and determination to win at all costs. You may not have felt like a warrior on any given day that you were wearing that game face—maybe your knee was acting up, or you were sick, or you just had a fight with your significant other or parents—but you wore it because it became a defense mechanism to which your body, and your opponents, would respond.

While a sense of self-confidence is important to have outside of sports, you can't pretend to be something you're not with people who are trying to help you get into your next role. Don't pretend to be excited about an opportunity if you're not. If your uncle is offering you a job at his auto-parts business, ask yourself: is this creating an opportunity for me, or closing doors? Obviously, if you have bills to pay and ballooning debt, you need to address that as quickly as possible, and if that is the only job on the horizon, you need to be responsible and take it. And if you take it, you give it your all—even while you are still looking toward the horizon to see what's next.

Remember that not every job will be your dream job, but keep a lookout for an opportunity to assume a role that could serve as a stepping-stone to something you would eventually like to do. For instance, people who are interested in broadcasting might have a goal of being in front of the cameras or in front of a radio mike. But would a position as an assistant producer be a good place to start? It would teach you the business, and give you good connections. While production may not be your life, loving the industry itself might be a good start. Walk with your eyes and ears—and mind—open.

Another person might wish to help out with a nonprofit, but a job opening is available for a charity that they don't identify with as much as some others. However, the experience at any nonprofit is invaluable if that's where you seek to be.

Chapter Three taught how answering simple questions about what you value with yourself, and others, you can reveal your authentic self. Remember to carry your Coins around with you to remind you what it is that you value. Also, remember to be a Coin collector: ask great questions.

## Acknowledge your Shortcomings

When I was first drafted, I had so much to say, so much pent-up energy! I couldn't wait to show my team all my talents. I wanted to meet the coach, meet the owner, meet everyone associated with the team, and show them that I had great things to contribute. That worked great until I was put on the spot, and then I couldn't think of what I wanted to say and why.

I realized that this was an area I needed to grow in, so I took an honest look at myself and realized that my communication skills in front of executives were not great. I had to develop a way to reduce my anxiety so that I was as comfortable speaking to the GM as I was speaking to my teammates.

What do you need to work on? Is it your presentation skills, showing up on time, your computer skills, or your ability to listen more carefully? Are you a procrastinator? It is easy to hide and we do a great job of it as human beings—especially athletes. We don't like for people to know that we don't know something, so sometimes we just go along as if we do. We have to learn to become more transparent. It's okay to admit you don't know something; when you ask, you learn. We are always coached to step up . . . so step up!!!

### Ask the Right Questions

I'm going to add an additional tenet to Troy's list: ask the right questions.

In the business world, asking the right questions is a huge key to success. One of the ways interviewers can trip you up is to ask: Do you have any questions for me? If you don't, it could be the difference between you and someone else getting the job. Absence of curiosity shows either disinterest in what you are doing there, a lack of foresight in researching the company that you're looking to work for, or that you haven't been listening enough to come up with intelligent follow-up questions.

A great question can impress the person you are engaged in conversation with, and allow that person the chance to follow through with a thoughtful response. After you have asked your great question, listen to all of what the person has to say. When we're engaged in a conversation, oftentimes we can't wait for the other person to stop talking so we can jump in and make our point or tell our story. I implore you to allow people to finish what they are saying. When you do, you it gives the speaker confidence that you think that what they have to say is worth listening to. Your job is to make the other person look like a superstar.

## Focus on Things You Can Control

One of the fastest stress relievers out there in transition is to maintain your focus on what you can control. If a decision is out of your hands, and you've done everything you can do, take your mind away from it. Focus on something else. Build your skill sets. Work on growing your team (see Part Three). Do something positive every day for your transition. We all have the power to control our state of being. We have the power to control our thoughts. I want you to smile big right now, and try to be sad at the same time. Now I want you to frown and try and be happy at the same time. It can't happen, right?

What are some activities that you do now to stay in the game or keep stress at bay? I love to exercise, eat right, study God's word, bowl, read a book, ride my bike, play golf, and work out with my daughter Lindsey to keep a rein on stress. What do you love to do?

## Going Outside the Box

Tracy Perlman might be the most powerful woman in the NFL, where she is the Vice President of Entertainment and Player Marketing. I've sat in meetings with Tracy, and although she is a petite woman in a sea of tall men, she can more than hold her own with her vibrant, smart, and dynamic personality. I asked her to give us some examples of players who took risks once their time in the NFL was over, and weigh in on some crucial transition advice.

> *You're so focused on playing the game when you're a professional player, it's hard to think about life after the NFL. We like to celebrate the guys who played America's Game, and we want them to stay engaged after they retire, participate in NFL events. We host opportunities to get former players together and engage with one*

*another and keep them engaged with us.*

*In transition, you've got to listen off the field as much as you listened when you were on it. There are people there to help you. A lot of guys need to reach out and talk to other guys. You were a member of a team, and so you now need to find people you trust to listen to. Most guys won't ask for help, but they do need help figuring out what their vision is for what's next. There are so many opportunities out there in the world, and it's time to study, figure it out, and listen.*

*I connect with guys as they're playing and once they're done playing, and I ask them what they are interested in doing. It's like looking at a road map—in what part of the world do they want to live? Do they want to coach, become a speaker, help other guys?*

Here are a few of Tracy's examples of people who went outside the box of how they were perceived on the field.

Jake Plummer was a quarterback for ten seasons, playing for the Cardinals and the Broncos, until he abruptly retired. When he left the game, he was burned out on the NFL and really didn't want anything to do with it anymore. He got into mountain biking, became a handball champion, and used his huge competitive streak in other venues. Tracy called him to come in and meet with her to explore possibilities of what they could do together, hoping to re-engage him with the game he played for so long. She promised, "If you hate it, and you're miserable, then you don't have to do anything else for us." She sent him to be a Heads' Up Football ambassador in Alaska, spreading the message of youth football safety. He wrote an op-ed after that, talking about how that experience helped him with that transition. Now he's analyst for the Pac-12 network.

Arian Foster is a running back for the Houston Texans, and also knows that he wants to act. He and Tracy connected and she was able to get him some experience: he played himself on *Hawaii Five-0* and played the part of a running back in *Draft Day*, which Tracey helped make sure accurately reflected the NFL.

Emmitt Smith was really tough when he was a player. He

didn't want to do anything off the field to detract him from his game. When he could no longer play, he wasn't sure what he was going to do. Tracy got him a gig on *Dancing with the Stars*, and he became hugely popular, winning the show's third season. "On the Thanksgiving Day Parade float, thirteen-year-old cheerleaders were going nuts for him," Tracy said. Emmitt admitted that he didn't really believe that he would have a whole new fan base, but his turn on *Dancing with the Stars* gave him a chance to be competitive and showed another side of his personality to a large part of the viewing public.

Drew Brees, quarterback for the New Orleans Saints, really wanted to connect with the men and women in our armed forces, so he got hooked up with the USO and went to Afghanistan, Iraq, and Guantanamo Bay to visit the troops. Now the Drew Brees Dream Foundation provides care, education, and opportunities for families and children in need, and works to improve the quality of life of cancer patients.

I always wanted to be in a movie, so I auditioned and landed a speaking role in the movie *Radio* with Cuba Gooding, Jr, Ed Harris, and Alfre Woodard. I also had a speaking role on the TV show *One Tree Hill*. Being inside a single box does not allow you the opportunity to maximize your potential; you must step outside of it to see what else is out there for you to try.

## About Courage and Risk

It takes courage to venture into unknown territory. I love reading stories in the Bible about how God used the internal fear of many people and transformed them into courageous leaders.

> *Be strong and courageous. Do not fear or be in dread of them, for it is the LORD your God who goes before you. He will not leave you nor forsake you.*
>
> *Deuteronomy 31:6*

Courage is the ability to overcome the discomfort created by the occurrence of fear. Courage gives us the strength or fortitude to also face fear, pain, uncertainty, and intimidation.

Courage comes from no known point; there is no system or innate chemical in our body that gives us courage. It is delivered from our belief system and our ability to reason through problems with emotional intelligence. If your emotional intelligence guides you to a certain point of reasoning that overcomes the perceived negative, a decision will be made. If your emotional intelligence cannot guide you to a decision one way or the other through analytical balancing, you are likely to do nothing. The important thing for you to understand is that you have made a decision, even when you decide to do nothing.

Sometimes the difference in assessing any situation is hope. Hope borders on what we think we know to be possible. Hope fights fear and creates courage. There are different degrees of hope; some are blind and some are just an inkling of faith. Hope is an emotion that creates attachment to the desired result. If we attach hope too early, we may take outrageous risk, because we just *want* something to happen. Think about this, pure and simple: wanting something doesn't make it happen. Need doesn't make it happen either. The process of critical thinking is the most likely way to increase your chances of getting from Point A to Point B.

### The Importance of Critical Thinking Skills

We will all go through life having to make some critical decisions. The problem with having to make critical decisions is that they usually don't come with a perfect amount of time in which to consider them. They make us very uncomfortable and may even cause our well-designed plans to change.

In sports, we learn to master critical thinking skills during meetings, practice, and the game, but when we transition from sports, it's as if we forget that we once possessed this critical area of thinking. So the questions are: Do you know what some critical thinking skills are? Do you believe you possess critical thinking skills? All of us naturally possess certain critical thinking skills, but the key is to be able to access them in a split second.

When we know decisions have great consequences, we are likely to think and analyze harder. This skill could be at your fingertips with just a little coaching. You will have to practice to accomplish the skill.

With any crucial decision, if you want to increase the likelihood of making a choice that results in accomplishment, you need to learn to automate your critical thinking skills. You want precise, meticulous, comprehensive information and investigation. You want to remove emotion from the thought process and reason with practical intelligence.

Temporarily put aside the belief systems we discussed in Chapter 1 and put on a new hat. Under this hat there is no thought of hope, loyalty, or desire, just pure analytical ability: a hard-core, raw skill. Consider the following types of decision makers:

- The risk-taker pursues the unknown for the hope of reward.
- The pacifist pursues habit for the sake of stability and complacency.
- The critical thinker seeks truth and discerns whether a path is worth pursuing.

In the moment of decision, the critical thinker has clear advantages. Our belief systems repeatedly cloud our judgment and potentially lead us to results that we neither expect nor desire.

When emotions—desire, attachment, loyalty, hope—play a part in your decision-making process, your reasoning and analytical skills can become cloudy. For instance, you make a decision to buy a house. You look at your existing finances and predict your income and determine that and the limit of what you can comfortably afford is $190,000. But the house you really *want* is $230,000, so you bid $200,000. Now you are attached by your desire to own the house, even knowing that it is over your budget. The owner counters at $215,000. You counter at $205,000, even more over your budget. The owner comes down again at $210,000. Are you willing to say to yourself, *I can't have it* and move on, or do you ignore your boundaries and go for it because you really want that house? This is an example of attachment. Great negotiators will teach you that *detachment* is the key to negotiating.

Another situation is weight gain. You do not gain fifty pounds at one time; you gain it over time; a half a pound or a pound a week. You make decisions to eat what you want, and decisions to not exercise. This happens one small decision at a time, rather than by one cataclysmic decision, but before too long, all those small choices lead to a very noticeable change. If you had been able to detach from your desire and look at the facts and the patterns of your behavior, you might have been able to visualize that there was a greater danger approaching, and made different small decisions along the way. This requires great honesty, self-awareness, and some level of accountability.

In any set of circumstances, there are things you can control, and things you cannot. Your actions and your emotions are within your control. External circumstances—such as the actions and emotions of others, forces of nature, and the whims of society—are beyond your control. When you have taken time to consider the many possibilities that are beyond your control, you can manage your expectations and your emotions so that no matter what the external circumstances end up being, you are internally prepared to work through them.

Should you balance the positive consequences against the negative consequences and see which one has the most gain? Should you rely on your "gut" or intuition? Maybe you should make a decision driven by your desires without regard to consequence? None of these is correct in critical thinking. Critical thinkers think in terms of *cause* and *effect*. A critical thinker considers the facts of a situation, then says, *If I do this, these are the things that will happen.* Removing emotion from your analysis of the situation is the key to making a decision that will produce the desired effect.

Now let's apply the same concept to a decision that is outside the scope of your expertise. You want to build a house, and stay within a certain budget. You have no expertise in construction, engineering, or any skills that pertain to the crafts involved in building a house. Do you figure that to save money you can skip the expert consultation, and that you can do it yourself? Or would you downsize the square footage so that you could afford the expert consultation? You must place value on each of the components and variables of the scenario. How much risk are you willing to take to satisfy your desires?

How does this work in a transition decision? Are you at greater vulnerability during transition times? If you have an inaccurate vision of your circumstances and needs, trouble may be coming. For instance, if you have finished professional sports and you are starting a new career or business, how do you envision your new income? We all want to think that we would keep the decision and desires in balance and have reasonable expectations. This is where starting over isn't easy. You desire achievement at the same level that you have previously accomplished. We have to hope for the best in ourselves, but the best in ourselves will come with accurate vision and prediction rather than in a cloud of hope. I'm not taking away hope, but I am challenging you to realistically manage your expectations.

In my transition from the NFL, I had to learn how to manage me. In learning how to see myself, I also learned to be practical in my decision-making processes and keep the decisions SMART: Simple, Measurable, Attainable, Realistic, and Time-bound. The NFL was big in my life, but my life is bigger than the NFL. Don't give your past so much credit than it drowns out your future potential.

### The Elements of Critical Thinking

Critical thinking includes a complex combination of skills, and the wisdom to apply those skills appropriately to any given set of circumstances. Critical thinkers must have:

**Knowledge.** We require a knowledge base to think critically. What do you know to be true about this situation? A critical thinker must gather factual information, often within a small amount of time. Critical thinkers understand that they must rely on current evidence rather than merely on the past, personal experience, or hearsay.

**Self-awareness.** To be in a state of self-awareness we must be able to step outside of our egos and look at our emotions without emotion. Critical thinkers accurately evaluate the influences of their own motives, and recognize and acknowledge their own assumptions, prejudices, filters, biases, and point of view.

**Rationality.** Rationality allows us to look upon our own situations as an observer. Critical thinkers consider evidence with reason instead of emotion. In the process of achieving rationality, a critical thinker removes the cloud of confusion and replaces it with explanation and quantifiable fact.

**Honesty.** Emotional impulses and selfish motives create self-deception. For a person to be honest with integrity, they must see the situation for what it is, not for what they want it to be. Honesty cuts through the layers of false perception and gets to the truth, whether it is pleasurable or painful.

**Open-mindedness.** Open-mindedness involves consideration. Are you able to consider the situation from different perspectives? Can you gain understanding by looking at the situation from another's point of view? Do you always have to be right? Is it ok with you to not have an answer?

**Discipline.** Keeping the critical thinking process consistent and sustainable requires discipline. A critical thinker holds themselves accountable for meticulous analysis of the facts.

**Judgment.** Judgment requires the ability to weigh or value the evidence available. Critical thinkers only make a decision after careful consideration of the facts. At the same time, they are already looking ahead to the potential effects of their decision, and planning for future decisions that may arise as consequences of this choice.

Critical thinkers:

- are skeptical by nature. They approach everything with the same analytical skepticism and suspicion.
- are active, not passive. They ask questions and analyze internally. They apply tactics and strategies to problem solving and ventures. They seek true meaning and understanding.
- are not egotistical or self-centered. They are willing to change their beliefs and objectively analyze data. They understand that facts must be interpreted.
- are intelligent. Accurate analysis requires the intelligence to interpret data, facts, emotions, and the surrounding scenario.

Non-critical thinkers:

- take a simplistic view of the situation.
- see black and white or yes and no without regard to creativity. They play the "all or none" game.
- fail to see links and cannot get through complexities.
- underestimate or overestimate related elements or evidence. They believe they know what evidence is relevant and take their facts only from that evidence.
- are egotistical and judgmental.
- generally consider only their own perspective.
- pursue their goals as the only pertinent and valid goals.

Which one would you rather be? Which one are you based on what you just read?

**Journal:**

How does it feel when you're around people who are authentic? Are they more accepting, more believable? What are their characteristics?

_____

_____

_____

_____

_____

_____

_____

_____

Do you believe that you are a critical thinker? Why or why not?

_____

_____

_____

_____

_____

_____

_____

_____

What does it mean to you to be a risk taker?

_____

_____

_____

_____

_____

_____

_____

## PART THREE:

## BUILDING YOUR IDEAL LOCKER ROOM

In 1997, Jim Lippincott, the long-time director of football operations for the Cincinnati Bengals, called me and said, "Leonard, we are not signing you back to the team." Translation: *You're done here, pal.*

My daughter, Lindsey, was just six weeks old. I was a brand new dad with a whole lot of responsibilities. I got off the phone, paralyzed, and instantly went into prayer. I told my wife Chandra that I had just been fired. We were both angry. I felt as if I had given so much to that team and the Cincinnati community over the past five seasons. It was an instant feeling of abandonment in a time when I needed the team…oh yeah, and the money with a new baby.

It's OK to be angry and disappointed when you receive bad news. It's also OK not to understand the reasons why. I wonder at times if we will ever know the WHY behind most things that happen in our lives?

Later that night, I prayed again. "Okay, Father, I'm going to show them that they made a mistake." I decided to create a new level of discipline. This was the time to use the hurt and fear of the unknown, to turn them into fuel. Faith comes without seeing. I had to leverage all those things that were going to propel me to my new destination, my new purpose. I knew I had a daughter to feed, so I had to pray harder, trust more, and work out harder and smarter than I ever had before.

I couldn't allow one team not wanting me to dictate to the

thirty others in the league at that time. One team's trash is another team's treasure. Cincinnati was one chapter in my life, and now it was time to write a new one.

When the Vikings signed me as a free agent, I told the chaplain of the team, Keith Johnson, "I didn't come here to make any friends. I don't want a TV in my room to keep me entertained. All I want to do is study the Bible, study my play book, and make the team."

I leveraged my adversity at being cut from the Cincinnati Bengals to work harder than I ever had before in my life. My friend Rich Campe warns people around me now, "Do not say anything negative to him. Don't tell him what he can't do. Overload with him with compliments. Because if somebody doubts him, he'll use it as leverage to conquer."

While it can be valuable to take the negative and use it to push yourself to a better place, this story comes with a warning: don't think you can use something negative to motivate yourself all the time. Create excellence and greatness for the purpose of creating excellence and greatness, not just out of spite or because someone challenged you to step up.

Part Three gives you a number of methods for creating a great and exciting new path for yourself. I have shared these tools over the last fifteen years with the people I coach privately, in speeches and to corporations in workshops. I'm so excited to present them to you in this book.

**Chapter Seven:**

## CREATING STRUCTURE:
## YOUR NEW TEAM

*No man is an island, entire of itself.*

*—John Donne*

When you're in transition, it's OK not to have all the answers. It's OK to know that you don't know what's next for you in life. I understand that it can be scary and exciting all wrapped up in one ball of anxiety.

Don't allow pride to keep you from seeking out people who can help you get what you need—or even just brainstorm ideas. Sometimes fear and doubt can drown you, because you don't want people to know you can't do it alone.

One day, I was moderating a panel for the NCAA, asking different players about their transition for a group of NCAA administrators. I asked one of the panelists to talk about his transition out of the NFL. He said, "Man, my transition was *hard*. There were nights when I was depressed—so depressed I was contemplating suicide."

I asked, "How did you get past that?"

The former player said, "I didn't want to be around people for a long time." His self-worth was shifting—people stopped asking for autographs, he stopped being recognized and lauded. But one day, he started trusting a single person enough to let him know what was really going on with his life. That led to him being able to trust another person. Slowly, this player kept reaching out and trusting until he had a new team of people who could help him find a new path in his life. The type of path he was looking for was one where he could achieve and shine in this emerging identity. This was going beyond the locker room at its best.

Eugene Robinson is a former player who was fortunate enough to have a mentor throughout his NFL career. His mentor taught him to always be looking forward, preparing for transition even as he prepared for each game.

*My transition from the NFL started as soon as I entered into the league back in 1985 for the Seattle Seahawks. I met a family man named David Brown. Dave was a ten-year veteran corner at the time, a God-fearing man who took me under his wing. His accomplishments were outstanding. He ended up with 62 interceptions (8th on the NFL all-time list), and received a Super Bowl ring with the Steelers.*

*Dave taught me how to watch film. There is indeed an art to watching football with an editing and critical eye in order to game plan and play your optimal best. Football is an academic game played with physicality and athleticism. I spent Wednesdays and Thursdays after practice at Dave's home, breaking down film. What a tedious process. Did I mention this was on VHS, at least three games, with two views from the sidelines and the end zone? I collated and parsed information like a surgeon repairing a torn Achilles tendon. At the end of a film session, I had to regurgitate every tendency, pattern, and nuance I found. Who knew that God was using Dave to teach me the secret to longevity in the NFL? I sure didn't. I had no clue to how long I would play (it ended up being 16 years) or how well I would play (57 interceptions, 3 Super Bowl appearances, 3 Pro Bowl appearances and a couple of All Pro designations).*

*Dave's mentorship was priceless, even before I understood what it was. I was learning the academics of football and had no clue if I would even be in the league the following year. Because my mentor was concerned about my welfare, he taught me everything*

*I would need to transition out of football long before I needed it. I soaked up everything I could from Dave like a sponge. I started to emulate his mannerisms. Dave was the players' chaplain and go-to guy for the team with the media; he spoke extremely well and could explain football to the novice. When Dave was traded, I became that guy. Dave even taught me how to make a financial plan that would serve me and my family my whole life.*

*God used my mentor to aid me and transition me. Dave passed away about nine years ago, and it was a very sad day for his family and my own. His wisdom was invaluable and his self-lessness was constant. He loved me and treated me as his son. I am still blown away when I think of how much he and his wife, Rhonda, poured into our lives.*

Remember who we had on our team in the locker rooms of our past? Back then, we couldn't choose our coaches, we couldn't choose the other players—they were chosen for us.

Do you want to know the great news about this part of your life?

Now, you get to choose who you want to be on your new team beyond the locker room. Remember those guys you didn't really enjoy being around in the locker room? They're gone. You no longer have to tolerate those who used to drive you crazy on your personal team. I put emphasis on your *personal* team and not every team that you are associated with in your transition.

So, who do you need on your team? You do need a diverse group of people. And you don't just need people you would honestly label as yes-men and women—these are people who don't challenge you to be your best.

Surround yourself with people who can support you in your transition, and assist you in your new life's journey. People who have your back. As Lee Corso said in a speech once in Charlotte, "Someone who doesn't just take cookies out of the cookie jar, but replaces them." Look within your own circle of influence to help build your new core team, but also seek advisors/mentors outside your regular circles as well.

## Types of People You Need on Your Team

rc h

There is a variety of people you need to have on your transition team to help you find your new path. Some might seem obvious, while others are intentionally there to shake things up.

### Mentor

> *There are friends who destroy each other, but a real friend sticks closer than a brother.*
> —*Proverbs 18:24*

That scripture, to me, describes what a mentor is.

In mythical writing, every great hero has a mentor. King Arthur had Merlin, and Mentor advised Odysseus in "The Odyssey." This figure is as old as time, and present in modern stories as well, like Obi Wan to Luke Skywalker, or Mr. Miyagi to the Karate Kid. Mentors are wise; they excel in life (sometimes quietly and humbly), and therefore provide inspiration and motivation. You aspire to be like them in most ways, and achieve what they have achieved. They don't have to be a generation older, they just need to have walked in your path and understand how difficult it is to be in transition. They are good at drawing from their life experience to help you clear your path for true direction.

In 2000, just after I had blown out my knee, ending my football career, I was asked to speak at a baccalaureate for a high school in Charlotte. After the ceremony, a man came up to me and held out his hand. "Hi. My name is David Gandy. You gave a great speech." He gave me his card and we shook hands. He told me he had a sports marketing company.

"I love marketing," I said, and made plans to call him the next week. He's been my mentor ever since. We call ourselves Ebony and Ivory: he's an older white gentleman with gray hair and I am a middle-aged caramel brother with short hair. While we have done some business together, he's been there for me more as an adviser and a great friend.

David is my mentor, and I've seen him win in his family life, in his business life, and with his friends. I've seen him overcome prostate cancer. I've seen him and his family build a successful car dealership. I've seen him win in his spiritual life. When you know God has brought you to someone, you need to stick to the relationship. Others might not understand what you have with that person, and think they can bring something different or better, or know what's best for you. You've got to stand firm, and stick with who you believe the Lord has brought within your new circle of influence to help sharpen you.

> *For our struggle is not against flesh and blood, but against the rulers, against the authorities, against the powers of this dark world and against the spiritual forces of evil in the heavenly realms. Therefore put on the full armor of God, so that when the day of evil comes, you may be able to stand your ground, and after you have done everything, to stand.*
> —*Ephesians 6:12-13*

Mentors are known for giving it to you straight, and that's how it should be. They are likely busy with their own successful lives, so you have to be cognizant of that fact and not waste their time when you get together or talk. On the flip side of the equation, a good mentor will not waste your time coddling you with feel-good praise, because they need to be informing you in the ways of the world.

A mentor has to be strong enough to tell you the truth. And you have to be strong enough to receive their message. The hardest thing I ever heard in my life was when my mentor David said, "I'm disappointed in you."

I asked him, "Why?"

"Because you haven't lived up to your potential in my eyes."

That was a real moment for me. David had called me out, and his disapproval brought tears to my eyes. I felt like I was doing *something*, but inside I knew it was not enough. I knew I could have been doing more. It took me a couple of days of moping around with my feelings hurt before I took some action, but very quickly after that I ramped up my efforts. I pursued my passion for speaking, motivating, and executive coaching. I got certified in as much as I could. I even went back to school and earned another degree.

Getting called out is hard, but you have to be open to that kind of hard-hitting advice, or you won't benefit from having a mentor. You're wasting their time and yours. David took a risk in losing his friendship with me by speaking honestly about what he saw happening with my life, but these last fourteen-plus years he's helped me to be a better man. I love you, brother!

Many coaches in my life have served as mentors as well, whether it was for a season, or thirty years and counting. When I was at Troy University in Alabama, my defensive back coach Mark Fleetwood told me, "When you get to the NFL, be a great special teams player." I didn't understand what that meant at the time. Why wasn't he telling me to be a great defensive back, which was my position? But then I figured it out: if you want to stick around on the team, accept the small but crucial roles. Be humble enough to learn how to be valuable and show that you want to stick around. It's like being an intern for a major corporation: you need to learn a craft quickly, and make yourself invaluable so that they want and need to hire you. Be OK with not being the leader at times but learning how to be led instead. Knowing your role and playing it to the fullest is crucial in transitioning.

## The Mentor Ask Process

If you don't know anybody in your circle who you would consider asking to be your mentor, and you're thinking of starting a business, the Small Business Administration (SBA) has a great list of places where you can find a mentor. There are also organizations that offer mentors for women, minorities, and veterans; trade organizations have them, too. You can also look within your own sphere of people.

When you've identified somebody you might want to ask to be

your mentor(s), ask to schedule a meeting. Let them know what you are looking for in a mentor (write it down), and with what issues you need help. See if you can set up a structure for your relationship, and have regularly scheduled meetings centered on questions and answers, the actions that you are taking, and the results you are or aren't getting.

Without Coach Rodney Walker, I wouldn't be where I am today. Hands down, he opened up a world of opportunity to me. My senior year of high school, I didn't have much direction as to what I would do after high school. Coach Walker personally drove my cousin and me in a van, from Toccoa, Georgia, to North Carolina to visit Lees-McRae College. It was the only school that had any interest in me. I received a little scholarship money, my parents took out a student loan, and I started my college football career there. In 2013, I was so proud to be inducted into the Lees-McRae hall of fame.

I probably wouldn't have gone to college if it hadn't been for Coach Walker. He changed the scope of our entire community, because with his encouragement, ten guys went to college our senior year to play football. I ended up at Troy University two years later, and got drafted into the NFL because of Coach Walker's selflessness. We are still in touch after all these years, and get together for dinner when we can. Thanks, Coach!

When I was in Cincinnati playing for the Bengals, Jeff Patton was the chaplain for the team. He loved the players and would always ask me to meet him on Tuesday, (which, by the way, is your ONLY day off in the NFL). I would always look at him like, "Dude, back up." I thought he was too pushy. But in 1994, he led me to Christ on one of those Tuesdays. Make sure that you make yourself available for your life to be changed forever. Thanks, Jeff!

David Gandy, Coach Walker, Keith Johnson, Reggie Rice, and Jeff Patton are just some of the people who have orchestrated my direction in life and played a huge role as my mentors. They accepted the responsibility to take me under their wings and give me a life leadership course. Maybe the people in your life have never taken on the label of mentor, but they have played a vital role in your life's success. Make sure that you recognize them and let them know how important they are or were in helping design your life's journey.

## The Other Teammates on your Team

How does a general manager staff a team? They look for diversity in skills, and a huge level of competitive spirit and focus.

Every year, two hundred fifty college players out of a pool of over 60,000 are invited to an event called the NFL combine. Getting invited is an honor, so if you get that far in your college career, you want to make sure you go all the way. At the combine, you're evaluated physically, academically, and for character. They look at everything. You're getting interviewed; you're getting pulled on every ligament and bone, and evaluated mentally. You take an intelligence test, similar to an SAT, called the Wonderlic; it tests your verbal and math skills. (Some people think that all football players can do is run, throw, and catch, but try a sample test online and you may have newfound respect for what the players must pass.) At the combine, you are in front of every owner, every general manager, every coach—so there couldn't have been a more important stage for me to display my skills than when I attended the NFL combine in 1992. Unfortunately, things did not go my way: running my 40-yard dash, I pulled a hamstring. After that, I couldn't do any of the drills that had been set up to test me (although I could do the bench-press, the vertical jump, and the standing broad jump). Here I was from this small school, and I'd lost my chance to show how I could excel. Adversity became very real to me.

But the Lord allows us to experience adversity because it develops character and perseverance. And he also creates other ways to sometimes achieve better results. We will not always know the Why behind every adversity or challenge.

Moses was getting ready to go into the Promised Land and God instructed him to speak to the rock for the Israelites and animals to have water to drink. Instead, he struck the rock with his rod twice, and because he didn't listen to directions, he was never allowed to experience the Promised Land.

Life's little instructions are what we need to do in order for us to experience our promised land. Everybody's pursuit to his or her promised land is different. I believed God had prepared me for this combine adversity; this was what he allowed to happen. I was so adamant that I was going to get drafted, that I thought, *Well, I guess that means they're just going to have to come to* me *to see me run at Troy.* And this came true. I ran for twenty different scouts over eighteen days in the weeks after the combine. Coach Ron Meeks gave me my hardest workout of all time, and the one who tested me so much ultimately became my defensive back coach for the Bengals.

When you're transitioning into a new role and building up the team that will support you in that role, you need to make sure you have both diversity and a level of focus that is different from what you had. It's easy to surround ourselves with people just like us who have had the same experiences and come from the same background. But that would be counterproductive. We need people who are different, who don't think like us at times, and who have different skill sets than we do.

For instance, on a college sports team, the players on your team might think more like you and look like you. They all might have different backgrounds—you could be playing with somebody from the suburbs, and someone from the city, someone from the Northeast, and someone from out West. So you think there is diversity there, but because you all share the same goal, you all have one common concern—to win. So you are not a very diverse group in terms of goals.

But let's look at the students who are outside that locker room—their goal setting is not on a game, it's on the *world*. Their focus is not on the internal world inside the locker room and out on the field—it's outside of that stadium.

Along with at least one mentor, your team should include:

*The Spiritual Leader*

As I've said in previous chapters, transitioning and going beyond can be a trying time for your ego, pride, and mental health. There's nobody who will put things in better perspective than a spiritual leader who helps us see our place in life.

Ask your friends and family for advice if you do not already have a spiritual home. Ask for meetings with various clergy members, and see who you click with and whose message resonates with you.

Andre Collins, who played for ten seasons in the NFL, credits Dr. Bill Theirfelder, who served as his sports performance coach midway through his career, as being the most valuable player on his transition team. "Bill had tremendous faith in God, as well as an ability to convey how important it was to focus on the task at hand. God has always provided me with great comfort. Even in my saddest, lowest moments, those tears and cries never fell on deaf ears. Bill helped plant that seed of hoping on God. In my life, because of that seed and what I know, everything is possible."

I was a churchgoer my whole life, attending every Sunday with my mom and sisters. But until 1994, I wasn't walking the walk—I was too busy working hard and playing hard. Jeff Patton, the chaplain for the Bengals, kept encouraging me to get together with him, but I kept feeling like he was trying to steal my thunder in hanging out with my friends and going to parties. However, I went with him to different speaking engagements at high schools, middle schools, and elementary schools, until one day, we met at a Bob Evans restaurant and right there, I gave my life to the Lord. Not soon after, in the preseason, I blew out my wrist and right there my faith was tested because I was placed on injured reserve and out for the entire football season in my third year as a pro. Chandra had moved to Cincinnati at that time and assisted me in getting back on my feet. My faith allowed me to sustain a higher level of strength in the midst of this dark time in my life.

*Faith is the substance hoped for and the evidence of things not seen.*

—Hebrews 11:1

I was still kind of a closet Christian, half in and half out, though, and in 1997 when I went to play for Minnesota Vikings, I was really first baptized by Keith Johnson, who was the chaplain for the Vikings. I had men like the great Reggie White, Pastor Reggie Rice, Randall Cunningham, Troy Vincent, and Cris Carter assist me at that time of my life and help me be a better leader on and off the field. They provided the correct level of accountability to be a better father and husband when I needed it. The spiritual teammates help us understand the value of serving others and how not to lean so much on the opinions of the world, but to discern when our creator is speaking to us.

### The Edgy Friend

We all have that friend who doesn't conform to the status quo, spots trends years before anybody else, and has a unique viewpoint on the world. They're the type of people who are reckless enough to curse in front of a pastor, but tear up at a Budweiser commercial. I like the edgy people; those jokers are provocative all the time. They'll tell anybody to shut up.

These people speak their minds and don't worry about hurting your feelings when you're still insisting on doing things the old way. They want you to open your eyes, see the world in a new way, and think outside the box. They are so honest that it hurts to converse with them at times because they are so opinionated. One of my edgy friends is my oldest friend, Elorado Cochran. He usually doesn't bite his words in our conversation, which allows us to have true transparency and real dialogue. Don't ignore your edgy friends; they can be the ones who are the best at helping you recognize the real you.

### The Street-Smart Teammate

Street-smart people have not lived in an ivory tower all their lives, with opportunities thrown at their feet from the moment they were born until the present day. These people have hustled to get where they are, and they have also seen some human behavior that would shock you. They have seen every scam known to mankind, and can smell a rat when all you can smell are roses. They will tell you how to look out for yourself in the real world, how not to get taken advantage of, and if you're lucky, will come along with you to meetings when you are close to deciding about making a business move. This teammate can raise red flags if he or she sees anything troublesome. If you are out with them, they can spot trouble while you're still thinking you're in the best place ever.

The street-smart friend is that voice that doesn't go along with everybody else's decision. This person has been taken advantage of before and usually provides some very discerning skepticism along your transition journey. As a former pro athlete, I have found myself in situations not really knowing if something is truly legitimate or a scam. We sometimes don't possess the life experience to draw from in order to make the best decisions, and without someone in our corner being a LOUD VOICE of reason, our naïveté can sometimes make us very vulnerable to deception.

### The Book-Smart Teammate

Book-smart people were the smartest in their class, and love nothing better than solving complex situations with research, research, and research. They can point out the best resources for you, and open your eyes to the greater world beyond sports.

While not all people who are book-smart are structured and follow the rules, it's helpful to find the teammate who crosses all the t's and dots all the i's. They are the people others make fun of in high school, but you may end up working for them later in life, so be careful who you're calling a nerd because they might be your boss one day.

### The Best Friend

I hope you have one (or two, or three) best friends in your life. They know how to be there for you and how to listen. They love you unconditionally, no matter where you are in your life, and you can depend on them to fly to the rescue no matter what time of day, month, or year it is, because you are important to them and they care about your happiness and well-being and ultimate success. They know what gets you up out of bed in the morning, and what kind of information crushes you. You can confide in them your deepest, darkest secrets, and they will still love you. I have been truly blessed to have some awesome godly men and women in my corner.

Pastor T. D. Jakes says that there are three types of people that you have in your life as friends.

*Confidants* are best friends, and will help you find your destiny, but you will have few of them. They are the people who will assist you to your end game in life. They invest back into your life. They are all in your business.

*Constituents* are into what you are into, but not into you. They are for what you are for. They will walk with you and work with you, but they are not for you. Don't mistake your constituents for confidants.

I liken this to if you've ever had really close friends from work, the locker room, or in the neighborhood. You get along great when you're together in your mission to make work a more fun place or the neighborhood a nicer place to live. But once you leave work or your street, these friends suddenly don't seem so interested in making the effort to see you, and this can be very depressing, unless you recognize their role as Constituents.

*Comrades* are against what you are against. They make strange bedfellows. They are not for you, not for what you are for. They fight a greater enemy in political situations, perhaps, or against a type of law you are against. They are with you until victory is accomplished. But after a while, they will desert you.

Be careful with whom you share your dreams, because Constituents and Comrades can't be trusted like Confidants. Thank the LORD for sending people to fulfill a certain purpose in your life. Who's on your team?

### Your Family Team

I'm going to throw this section over to my friend Hardy Nickerson, who writes about this so eloquently:

*The transition for my family was a little tough at first, but got better once they got used to my new role. For so many years we operated on the NFL calendar, and our way of life was defined by the NFL, such as times for training camp, Tuesdays off, etc. During the season, I would leave home around 6:30 a.m. and not get back until after 6 p.m. And I was hardly around on the weekends. So once I retired, I was home all the time and it was different for everyone. I think my kids really liked that I was around. I was suddenly able to help out with their school functions, field trips, etc. I helped out driving the kids around, which freed up my wife to do other things. So it was a plus in that I was able to spend time with my family. My wife welcomed my presence, but it did create some changes for her. She had been used to doing a lot of things on her own, and then I was around. But it wasn't really a bad thing. My relationship with my wife got stronger, we had more time to do things, go to lunch, etc. We also started working together and were our own team, which was very positive.*

*My wife and kids have always been in my personal huddle and that has not changed. They have remained constant and have always been very supportive of me. I don't have the same experiences now as I did when I was playing, in the sense of the huddle and the locker room, but my family provides positive support, encouragement, and love that feels like a team. We are definitely a team and operate like one.*

## The Difference Between a Man's Team and a Woman's Team

Women tend to have a better time than men in seeking out help and friendships and building consensus toward a future, but not all women are the same. Some women can be very easy to inspire and motivate, while others shrink at criticism. I grew up with three sisters and I witnessed them lose so many great friends due to a lack of trust. Women rely on sustained communication.

Men grow up hearing our friends call us dumb, whereas women don't grow up hearing that from other women, so when a woman hears "That's a dumb decision," she thinks her intelligence is being attacked, rather than that one decision. Be sensitive to the difference between men and women when asking for advice and receiving it.

Men, on the other hand, do a great job at hiding things that don't reflect well on us. So we hide our fears, our addictions, our doubts. We don't want to look like less than a man, but it's hard to get honest advice without being honest with those we are seeking it from.

For men and women, what it takes to give and get advice is love, respect, and trust. When you are respected you feel love, where there's love, there's trust. Open dialogue can only happen when those three things are flowing in unison.

**Journal:**

Why did you and your best teammate connect in the first place?

_____

_____

_____

What is the main characteristic of your best teammate?

_____

_____

_____

How do you find your best teammate outside of your sport?

_____

_____

_____

Do you have a mentor? Why is that mentor important to you?

_____

_____

_____

## Chapter Eight:

## UNDERSTANDING THE "WHY"
## BEHIND YOUR PURPOSE

*THE GREATEST TRAGEDY IN LIFE IS NOT DEATH, BUT LIFE
WITHOUT A PURPOSE.*

—*Reverend Myles Munroe*

Now that you've got your team in place, let's start identifying and aligning your purpose. Do you know the "Why" behind your purpose? Why did you play any sport growing up? Why did you desire to play in college? Why did you decide not to play in college?

Besides athletics, what are you here on earth to do? Don't allow people to feed you bull that all of your value comes from what you did in sports. Let go of the limiting belief that athletics is all that you have to offer. We all have dreams of becoming; so don't ever stop dreaming of becoming.

*I BELIEVE GOD MADE ME FOR A PURPOSE, BUT HE ALSO
MADE ME FAST. AND WHEN I RUN, I FEEL HIS PLEASURE.*
—*Eric Liddell, Chariots of Fire*

I played football for over half of my life, but I've always believed that I was more than just Leonard Wheeler the football player.

Football was never my God.

I started playing as a little kid, and I knew from a young age that I wanted to go pro. Even though I hoped to always do my best, I didn't want football to be who I was. I didn't want it to be the core of me, so how would I not allow that to happen?

My dad owned a pool hall in our town when I was growing up. He was an entrepreneur. This created an attachment for me that owning something was good; being an entrepreneur was good. My dad was not a great dad, but him being a business owner planted a seed in me that being your own boss is a good thing. (It is important for us to always see the positive in the midst of what seems to be a bad situation.)

The Lord has given all of us certain tools, but you as an individual need to continue to provide yourself opportunities to use the tools. This is done by making yourself available to be successful. One of the first commandments in Genesis is to till the fields: *Go out and work.* While professional athletes build the game for the fans, for ourselves, and our children's children, the people in the suites are building a legacy of ownership. That team is theirs. If I was expendable to them, it was pertinent for me to understand WHY.

We have to learn to create ownership. We have to look around and see what's needed in the marketplace. I think the main reason people don't create their own business is the fear of failure.

When I was a rookie with the Bengals, I decided to form a business with my friend in Atlanta. We bought a stretch limousine with a built-in VCR. This dates me, but back then, it was quite a luxury to have a video playing in the back of a car. I didn't know business; I just knew that I wanted success from something that I created. I knew the Bengals could cut me on any given day, and I needed to have something to fall back on. The business didn't last very long and I didn't lose any money, but the business learning experience was invaluable.

When I was still a rookie, I started speaking to high schools for Athletes in Action, and different Christian organizations. Those early days speaking were difficult at first—I was nervous, especially as a person who used to have a speech disability. But those days led to more engagements, and more attempts to practice and hone the way I speak and the messages I deliver, and now, twenty years later,

I am asked to train and speak all over the world.

I had a guy come up to me after my speech the other day. He said, "I've heard a lot of people speak, and you're right there up at the top. My son wants to become a speaker, do you mind if we call you?" It thrilled me to know that I had become inspirational, at least to this father and son. Just as I studied the great speakers when I knew I wanted to incorporate speaking into my post-athletic life, now I was one of the ones who was going to be emulated. When we played sports, we were aware that kids and others emulated our play. It doesn't change in your transformation stage.

It's important to remember, too, that you can take pieces from every life experience and create your own style from that. Don't ever feel like you have to be exactly like the other guy, because everyone brings something unique to the table.

If we go back to the first chapter about when you were a kid and your athletic talents started to be noticed by others, were there skills and pursuits that were sidelined in the pursuit of athletic excellence? Look back at the list you made.

Andre Collins is an 11-year NFL Veteran and NFLPA Executive Director for the PAF Professional Athletes Foundation; he assists current and former NFL players in their transition. He says:

> *I felt like I was on a tremendous track for academics. I loved to learn and explore. I enjoyed school, reading the paper. I enjoyed people and the things people say. When athletics began to dominate my time, I did just fine in school, but the physical commitment to football forced me to cut corners on my reading and learning. Today I still have poor reading habits and have to force myself to read and focus on learning. Today whenever I finish a book, instead of just saying "nice book," for me it is like winning the Super Bowl, because I never had the luxury of reading for leisure like I do today. I am curious again about learning and understanding, and not drawing quick conclusions because I'm pressed for time and energy.*

*I did not like how one-dimensional football was. The game did nothing to develop my sensibilities as an everyday man. Did nothing to develop my sensibilities as a father. Nothing to develop my sensitivities as a lover. Nothing to develop my ability to manage my senses and then compare my interpretation of things to how anyone outside of the game would interpret life.*

You can tell that Andre was frustrated at not being able to utilize all his skills when he was a full-time professional athlete. We are more diverse than we or others give us credit for, and we bring true value to everything we do. We have multiple gifts, many of which have been left untapped and remain waiting in limbo until we become more aware of our Why. When you are identifying your purpose, you are tapping into your full potential. It's hard for a person to tell me that they understand their purpose without using their potential.

Using the list from Chapter One, we're going to go further into exploring your potential and gifts, and how we can utilize those gifts for finding your purpose. This is a process, and the first stop along the way may not be what you expect.

## Who are You Serving? Finding an Objective

THE BEST WAY TO FIND YOURSELF IS TO LOSE YOURSELF IN THE SERVICE OF OTHERS.

—*Gandhi*

At game on Nation, where I am part of a team that leads workshops for sports groups and companies, we have a game called Objectives. The purpose of the game is to establish an objective before we speak with someone. For instance, when I'm speaking to a group, if my objective is to have the audience leave feeling inspired, I'm going to find those words that fit the objective, like *stimulated, moved, encouraged, motivated, passionate.* I'm also going to be deliberate about my stance—the way I stand in front of an audience—and my expression. Our physiology communicates up to 55 percent of how we communicate, and includes our facial expressions, posture, the way we stand, and even the way we mirror others. Our tonalities (the pitch of our voice, the loudness or softness of it) communicates 38 percent, and our words only 7 percent. Since so much of my message will come from things besides what I say, when my objective is to inspire an audience, the first thing I have to work on is presenting an inspirational physiology.

If you approach a situation—for example, a meeting—without taking the time to identify your purpose for being there, without a specific objective in mind, you're going to have to guess what you should do. And no matter what you do, when the meeting ends, you won't know whether you've accomplished your goal or not.

Let's say a father has an objective in his head: he wants his daughter to feel *motivated, enthusiastic,* and *encouraged,* so his language and physical presence need to match his objective. His language would be: *You are truly one of the smartest kids I know and I'm so proud of you. You can do what you want to do if you just work hard. Find what you love to do. Daddy's always got your back. If you fall down, I'll help pick you back up again.* His daughter would enter situations, opportunities, and relationships feeling encouraged, motivated, and enthusiastic about who she is.

Some people have this attitude: "I'm going to be who I am, and if they don't like it, that's too bad." To that, I counter with an emphatic: *No Way.* That's not a mature or realistic view of the world. If you're not willing to adapt, adjust, and shift your thinking to go along with the scenario you're in, you're not putting your purpose to work. For instance, if the father in the example above tries to hold on to an old objective to remain true to the way he was raised (sternly, with no encouragement, and no love), it is contrary to his new objective (to raise his daughter to feel motivated, enthusiastic, and encouraged). If he doesn't let go of the old to make room for the new, he will fail himself and his daughter. Don't be too prideful in adapting to what is needed.

My daughter, Lindsey, ran in the National Junior Olympics for USATF Track, and I needed to give her a life lesson about competition. My objective was to teach her to shift her state of being in order to compete at a higher level. She needed to show her competitors that she was fierce, and that state of mind had to match her stance, her posture, and even her walk. I told her, "You control your state all the time. If you're lying around on the couch, then it's fine to have a laid-back state. But if you want to be in control of your state and say *This is what I want, I'm going after it,* you will show enthusiasm in the drills you have to run." She shifted her on-the-track state to forceful, and she warmed up aggressively with her body, her mind, and her emotions. You can't act lethargic and be aggressive; the physiology has to match your way of thinking. There has to be congruence in your thoughts and behavior, when your inner and outer states are aligned. She needed the words to go along with her feelings: *I'm so pumped to be here today. I can't wait to get out there. I'm going to win this thing.*

This way of thinking is essential in your transition. You cannot change what you refuse to confront. If you really want to do something, you'll find a way. If you don't, you'll find an excuse.

We have between 40,000 and 60,000 thoughts each day. If 95 percent of your thinking is the same the next day, then you will have the same type of results from your day that you had the day before, unless you make an intentional decision to change. That's why it's important to control your state. If the way you do some things is the way you do most, it's only a matter of time before it catches up with you. You have to clear your way for new thoughts and new actions.

For instance, my dad used to say, "If I could just get out of this town…"—then his life would be different and he could unleash his potential. He warned me, "This town will eat you up." But I never saw him make a move to get out. Was it the town, or his state, that he couldn't control? It was clear that he allowed his environment to control his potential by not taking action. The environment can win, especially if you succumb to it.

This takes us back to the story of the Israelites in the book of Exodus, leaving Egypt and a life of slavery for their destiny in the Promised Land. They were able to change their environment, but they weren't aware that they were taking the same slavery-created, stagnant mind-set with them to the new Promised Land. In your transition, it is pertinent to understand that the way you think rules the way you act. Create awareness during your journey. Don't take the old into the new, unless it's productive and aligns with your new path.

A new town, job, relationship, and status in life—they all demand a new mind-set; you can't do the things the way you used to. We all know the definition of insanity: doing the same things over and over while expecting something to change.

The stories in this book show you that you are not alone, and that others have traveled this journey while leaving clues for you to take a better route without all of the pitfalls.

For instance, while my dad was telling me to get out of my hometown, my mother was helping me to control my mental and physical state with encouragements such as:

- "Fight your battles on your knees with prayer."
- "You can do anything you put your mind to."
- "If you don't believe in yourself, it's going to be hard to convince them."
- "Trust in the Lord. He's never going to let you down."
- "One day you're going to leave, and you're going to do great things."
- "Nothing is bad, it's a growth process."
- "We might be here right now, but maybe not tomorrow."
- "Come on son, get up."

My mother would come to watch my games when I was a kid and teenager. But she didn't just watch to cheer me on; she was watching me with intention. When I came off the field after the game, she would tell me what plays she thought I did great on, as well as where I needed to put in more work.

I learned to do the same with my daughter. When our children are playing sports or acting in a play or playing in a concert, we need to give them specifics of what they did great first, and then what they can work on to do even better. Just being there is not enough for your children, and it's not enough for your transition. Being *present* means both being there and being engaged with what's happening in your environment and the people in it. Being present plays an important role in your transition. Whether you are a parent, coach, teacher, employee, or owner of a company, sharing the specifics of what you observe allows the other people in your life to engage at a higher level.

## Don't be Expendable

The NFL Draft was one of the most brutal days of my life emotionally. I grew up playing sandlot football, starting at the age of four. I told my mom when I was eight that I was going to play pro ball and take care of her. I didn't realize what getting drafted meant at that age, but it planted a seed that would continue to be nurtured. Getting drafted at the age of twenty-two was my purpose at that time.

On the day of the NFL draft, I heard other players' names called before mine. My mind was racing: *I'm not good enough, and people I know who aren't as good as I am are getting drafted before me.* Finally my name was called in the third round, and my agent called to say that the Cincinnati Bengals wanted to sign me and that they were going to call. I felt a tremendous sense of relief that I had made my goal, and my purpose as an NFL player was going to be accomplished. But the reality was that I was still broke for the immediate future, and I didn't have a solution for how I was going to pay for my next meal, let alone send my mom some money to help out with her expenses.

So my new purpose was to make the team, and figure out what value I would add to the team so that I was not expendable.

EVERYBODY'S EXPENDABLE AT SOME POINT IN THEIR CAREER,
BUT WE HAVE TO FIND SOMETHING THAT WE CAN DO BETTER
AND LONGER THAN ANYONE ELSE.

After all, I had numerous people to please. I've always served the Father, and now I had to serve the owner, the general manager, the president of the team, the vice president, the head coach, the assistant coach, the special teams coach, my teammates, the fans, the journalists. Not to mention my family! Every athlete has to satisfy all of these hierarchical judgments.

My new objective after the draft became: *How do I make all these people happy?* Is it even possible? A pro athlete has a limited grace period for performing badly. I remember when I had a bad practice or game, I would come back into the locker room, and look around realizing that if it continued, I might not have that locker on Monday. Having to perform at a level of excellence for others outside of yourself can add excruciating pressure.

This thought haunted me many times during my NFL career. In training camp, in the middle of one night, I heard knocking on the door, and knew it was the scout coming to tell me it was time to go home—I no longer was on the team. But fortunately for me (and unfortunately for the other guy), it was the guy next door's time to hear those brutal words. The scouts were periodically out in the parking lot during the season, picking out one of my teammates and telling him, "I need your playbook: you're going home."

My objective once again: *Don't be expendable.*

### Ask the Question: What are My Strengths and Weaknesses?

People around you can see gifts and talents in you that you may not see in yourself. They can help you map out a larger picture of yourself than you see in front of the mirror. Ask people who know you well to be honest about what you do really well, and where you don't excel. Prepare yourself to accept their answers, good and bad. *Some potential feedback words:*

| | |
|---|---|
| team player | late |
| accountable | flirt |
| proactive | inappropriate |

| | |
|---|---|
| humorous | technologically gifted |
| friendly | big-picture thinker |
| intelligent | detail-oriented |
| well-read | good under deadline/pressure |
| researcher | fast learner |
| disciplined | technologically challenged |
| solid work ethic | math whiz |
| lazy | leader |
| disorganized | |

Gather the feedback and see if you can come up with a cohesive sense of your strengths and weaknesses. (Note: If you can't gather enough feedback from people you know, there are online quizzes, or you can work with a coach, or buy a book on this. See the resources section at the back of the book.)

### Turn Your Feedback into a SWOT List

Next, create a list of your Strengths, Weaknesses, Opportunities, and Threats. These lists are used for corporations, but can also be used for individuals. For instance, an opportunity could be that a business you want to create doesn't have any competition where you live. A threat would be if the business you wanted to enter into had a lot of serious competition, or was being heavily regulated, or was difficult to staff in a particular area.

### Making a Try-Out List for Success

Identify two or three items on that list that you want to work on, and give yourself a timeline, such as: *Over the next 48 hours I'm going to work on these two skills.* When that timeline is over, critique yourself fairly, not discouragingly.

For instance, a lot of ex-athletes think about going into broadcast journalism or coaching. But do your strengths include being articulate, knowledgeable, presentable, and quick on your feet? Do your skills involve motivating people and identifying solutions to problems? For the person interested in broadcasting, he/she could work on making videos of themselves and commentating on a game or a player. Someone interested in coaching could volunteer on a local team as an assistant, be it middle school, high school, college, or pro.

Your past builds your purpose; it builds the legs and arms to support your purpose. It builds your voice. I remember knowing answers to tests at school, but I was too afraid to raise my hand from a fear of stuttering out the answer. My stuttering wasn't as bad as my fear of speaking—so that fear became victorious, which in turn elevated my impediment. Yet I overcame that past to become a public speaker today. How have you overcome a fear?

*I LEARNED THAT COURAGE WAS NOT THE ABSENCE OF FEAR,*
*BUT THE TRIUMPH OVER IT. THE BRAVE MAN IS NOT HE WHO*
*DOES NOT FEEL AFRAID, BUT HE WHO CONQUERS THAT FEAR.*
*—Nelson Mandela*

I critique myself after every speech that I give on a scale from 1–10, on presentation, enunciation, and audience engagement. I also give the companies that hire me a form with which to critique me as well. As a football player, I was used to this self-critique in looking at the film of the games I played. How do you grow without looking at your film—and seeing how other people see you? These new critiquing sessions will be your film.

You can't go through your life pretending that your personal weaknesses don't exist, because they do. Undertake a mission to overcome your weaknesses and elevate yourself by self-evaluating or asking people you trust what they would say your weaknesses are. It is going to be important in your transition to identify your strengths, but to also expose your potential blind spots. This process allows you not to go into pursuing your purpose blindly, thinking that your talents fit every desired opportunity.

Your purpose will continue to change as long as you allow it to. It's not etched in stone; life is a journey. The people who aren't flexible on a team don't usually make it as far as they could if they allowed themselves the courtesy to be flexible. It is no different from stretching muscles in your body. They will become stronger and create more sustainable health when stretched appropriately.

Sometimes you can be too good in your own mind to take assignments you think are beneath you. You can also be the opposite and not take chances when you can handle it. Sheryl Sandberg's *Lean In* outlines how women often hold themselves back from taking assignments that men would readily volunteer for. Women don't volunteer if they didn't think they are qualified, whereas men will take the job and figure that they can learn the skills on the job. Sandberg encourages women to be flexible and not worry about being fully qualified 100 percent of the time for every job, because it's unrealistic to expect that of yourself.

When I spoke to students and professors at MIT for the first time, I was plagued by doubt. As much as I love Troy University, it's not MIT. So there I was with eighty students and a couple of assistant deans, speaking about leadership and communication. My self-talk sounded like this: *What can I offer them? These are little geniuses!* I was allowing old belief systems to play a role in my present success. Do not discount your life's experiences; learning is learning, regardless of where it's from. Everybody's story and wisdom can impart a wealth of knowledge into somebody else's world. The session was great and I even went back, thanks to my good friend Tammy Stevens (graduate and assistant dean of MIT).

> *The wicked man flees, when no man pursues: but the just,*
> *bold as a lion, shall be without dread.*
>
> —*Proverbs 28:1*

## Don't Limit your Gifts

> *I AM NOT AFRAID OF AN ARMY OF LIONS LED BY A SHEEP;*
> *I AM AFRAID OF AN ARMY OF SHEEP LED BY A LION.*
>
> —*Alexander the Great*

You can have more than one gift and purpose in life. You can be a coach, a doctor, a parent, a teacher, a cook, a landscaper, an entrepreneur, an advocate for change, and a friend. Your potential and purpose can be outlined in each one of those careers, and yet they all play a role in you becoming the person you are today. As much as I love speaking in front of people, I would be lost if I couldn't teach my weekly class at the YMCA, where I've been teaching for the past twelve years. I would be upset if I couldn't cook meals for my family and friends, because I love to serve others along with being creative in what I cook. Raising my daughter and training with her has been a real gift to me, so adjusting my travel schedule to make sure I have time for her and her activities is extremely important.

In the process of fulfilling your purpose and gifts, it's easy to get lost. You can forget about your purpose for being. You forget to walk as boldly as a lion. Speaking boldly is not going to sound humble. When you're trying to inspire and motivate, you've got to get in that state of mind where you are there to do a job and impart your knowledge.

You start to develop more gifts through your maturation process—these gifts always existed, but you didn't know how to use them before. Now you do.

Through life-learning experiences, you will continue seeing that your gifts have tremendous value. You need to recognize and appreciate these gifts and it will allow you to do the same when acknowledging the gifts in others. Somebody who was impatient and disorganized before being a parent develops the organizational skills of Martha Stewart after parenting small children. A woman who was shy and easily embarrassed gained wisdom with years of experience, so that her knowledge empowered her to no longer be shy in front of others. She realized that sharing her wisdom was more important than agonizing over the occasional flub.

Without the reinforcement of the crowd, the fans, the approval from playing sports, it's easy to get lost in thinking what you are or were doing is perfect. Feedback, both good and bad, allowed me to change some of my own thinking about myself. The feedback allowed me to view the critiquing as my film, which assisted in my maturation process and has continued to be valuable in my transition.

Felicia Hall Allen is an attorney who has worked as an executive for Nike, the NFL, and the WNBA. She reminds us to be open to the resources we have both within us and around us:

> *How we transition is a choice, and the risks we take will determine where we land. Advice: Don't go it alone, plan ahead, and trust God. Everything we need, we have. Learn to see opportunities in the places, people, and things that you once took for granted. We don't always see the things we need right away, but I am convinced that they are there. There is more to you than the accolades, trophies, or titles that others have bestowed upon you. Who you are isn't what you do.*
>
> *Transition is about purpose, joy, and confidence in knowing that you are where you are supposed to be, doing what you are supposed to be doing. Your circumstances can change but impact is determined by outlook and output. Enjoy the journey, and make the most of the tools that you have been given. You have them for reason. Use them.*

**Journal:**

What gifts are you not recognizing today?

_____
_____
_____
_____
_____
_____

What do people tell you that you are good at?

_____
_____
_____
_____
_____

I believe that we all have more than one purpose in life. What are yours?

_____
_____
_____
_____
_____

Why are you here?

_____
_____
_____
_____
_____

**Chapter Nine:**

## EIGHT CORE DISCIPLINES OF TRANSITION

Transitions are about discipline. Think about it: as athletes, we are conditioned to be very disciplined in our training and with our bodies. If you played football you practiced on the field, and when you weren't at practice, you watched films, and when you weren't watching films you were watching what you were eating, and when you weren't watching what you were eating you were working out, and when you were lying in bed, you were mentally running plays in your head. You were *always* preparing yourself for excellence on the field.

You have to keep up with the same level of discipline during your transitions. I'm calling them the core disciplines, because the core is the center of the athlete's body. Without a solid core, your body will crumble. When we were athletes, we were always talking about our core disciplines, because when your core disciplines break down, your game will crumble. Without a core to your family, your foundation breaks down in your home. An apple's core contains the seeds to the future. The core is everything.

What are some things in your life that break down your core disciplines? We all have our Kryptonite in life; we have to identify what it is. Sometimes it is partying, spending too much time working, spending more time reading than with your family, too much time in front of the television, too much junk food, or playing video games. Your Kryptonite is that thing that distracts you from capturing the essence of success—whether your desired success is health, wealth, spirituality, or strength of family. In college I started something to help me counter-balance my fitness regimen. If I partied on a Friday or Saturday night, the next day I would wake up and would absolutely destroy myself by putting my body through a grueling workout. I wanted to make up for what I did to my body and come back even stronger.

I challenge myself in different areas to make sure that I'm remaining strong and not allowing outside forces to control my mind. I do a health cleanse every four months to remove all the toxins from my body; I have to also do a spiritual cleanse as well to remove all the toxic people from my life.

Let's go into the eight core disciplines and see how they resonate with you.

## Core Discipline #1: Know What Your Foundation is Built Upon

I grew up in the church. Every Sunday we were there for Sunday school and then the big church service after. We were in vacation bible school in the summers. So my foundation was spiritual, but it did not secure my understanding as to what that meant to me as an adult. There's a scripture: *"Study to show thyself approved,"* (2 Timothy 15) which means that as an adult I need to know why I serve who I serve. I can't go off of what Mom and Dad said to be true to myself an adult. Even as a teenager, you need to know why you serve who you serve.

Why do you believe what you believe? How do you determine if your foundation is on good soil, and that whatever you plant there is going to grow? Knowing what your foundation is allows you to take the appropriate action in growing it some more. When you don't know what your foundation is, anywhere you go is the right place. Foundation gives support, and provides mentors.

*IT IS NOT THE BEAUTY OF A BUILDING YOU SHOULD LOOK
AT; IT'S THE CONSTRUCTION OF THE FOUNDATION THAT
WILL STAND THE TEST OF TIME.*

—*David Allan Coe*

The other day I was in a hotel room in San Francisco, preparing for a speaking engagement. I put on a gospel song and I was getting ready and doing the routine I go through before I speak. A song came on that really resonated with me, and I just stopped and I thought about giving thanks for everybody in my life. I felt unworthy and blessed that I'm chosen to do what I'm doing. Here I was, a small town boy from Georgia, being put up at a beautiful hotel, about to speak in front of amazingly accomplished business people. The essence of my foundation is always to be thankful, and give thanks and show appreciation for everything. I end every meeting with important people in my life with these words, "I appreciate you."

When your core discipline is spiritual it allows your reliance not to be on yourself so much. You're not so self-focused. Being spiritual teaches me how to love myself, which in turn gives me permission and direction in how to love others. It's truly hard for me to love others if I don't love me. If I hated myself, I would not be a pleasant person to be around. Believing in the power of God and His influence continues to be what feeds me in every part of my life. I will continue falling short of being perfect, but God's grace and mercy helps me to understand that I'm never alone in making decisions. What is your foundation and how would you discuss it with others?

## Core Discipline #2: Get serious about your Health

As Terry Crews, actor and former LA Rams player, said on *The Ellen Show* in 2014:

> *All your discipline is not discipline when you're a football player. There's always somebody telling you what to do. I'll never forget when I went to the gym for the first time after I retired, and I was like, "I want to work out," and they were, like, "OK, that'll be $30 a month." And I said, "What, you gotta pay?!" I mean, I had never paid to work out. I just decided, I'm gonna keep what I got. It is my spa therapy. Every time I go to the gym, I treat it like my moment, it's my time, I get my mind together—the whole thing.*

Athletes are brought up to take good care of their bodies in order to maximize their performance. Eating right and exercising are every bit as important as practice time. But I have seen athletes let themselves go after they are no longer required to keep in shape. Guys who could burn through thousands of calories when they were playing and had to eat to bulk up during their career start packing on the pounds when they are no longer exercising for hours at a time. Depression can factor into stealing your discipline to make it to the gym for a workout, or hit the streets for a morning run.

A lot of the successful people I know are disciplined about the way they take care of their health, because if they are feeling sleepy, or under-energized, or bloated, their performance at work will suffer. It's much harder to fit in workouts and eating healthy when it's not your job or your focus.

I was taught that you don't stay in the house and play. If it's not raining, you get out of the house. Growing up in the projects, we didn't have a lot to do, so we were very creative about ways we could have fun. We jumped off project houses onto old mattresses. We jumped out of trees to see who could jump the farthest. We had weightlifting contests at all ages; I started lifting weights when

I was five. We had running tests. Those were the core disciplines of health.

But kids today love to stay inside and play video games or hang out watching television because it's hot outside. There are some parents who allow the video games and television to act as a babysitter. Why not? It takes away you having to play with your kids. And others tell their kids to go play, but don't actually do anything active themselves. Would it really be the end of the world for you to be active like you're telling your kid to do?

That's why I love teaching my two NFL boot camp classes at the YMCA. We build camaraderie and discipline. My students hold me accountable to stay in shape, and I do the same for them. You cannot do it alone. I have people in my class from age sixteen to fifty-five, and we do extreme, over-the-top, brown bag exercises of sprints, heavy endurance weights, biometrics, calisthenics, and functional exercises. I challenge my students to make a commitment to be there and do their best, both mentally and physically.

How can you do anything without your health? Try to think of three things that you can do without being healthy. Well? I'm waiting. It's impossible to even rest or think properly if you're in pain, or you have difficulty moving or even catching your breath as you walk across a room.

There are some people who say: "I'm overweight, but who cares? I'm going to die some kind of way." That's a lie. Those people don't want to accept accountability for not making healthy choices. Everything is laced with the foundation of being accountable in this life to someone or something.

I grew up in the South, where we ate pork, cooked in lard, and fried mostly everything. But my mom cooked homemade, wonderful food every day. Sure, some of it was fried, but still, we ate a home-cooked meal. Health-conscious parents who feed their kids fresh spinach, avocado, organic fruits, and skinless chicken serve their bodies even better. When I became an high-performing athlete, I realized that the type of food that I truly loved as a boy would not help me achieve my athletic goals, so I learned more about nutrition and how to eat healthier. Today, I love cooking healthy and delicious foods for my family and friends. Sure, I splurge every now and then, but there is a foundation of nutrition that I always return to.

So if you say that you love and care about yourself, ask yourself: What's my level of love for myself, on a scale of 1 to 10?

1    2    3    4    5    6    7    8    9    10

Circle your number. If you circle 6, what are two things that you can do for you to be an 8 or 9? Write down two things that you can do over the next twenty-four hours to love you better. Examples:

- Wake up early
- Eat right
- Work out
- Find an exercise person to work out with or to train you
- Open those recipe books
- Google different recipes
- YouTube different workouts
- Eat to lower your genetically high cholesterol
- Walk a mile every other day

At the NFL, we have a community program called "Play 60." It encourages children to play outside 60 minutes a day. But this is true for adults as well. We were not designed to be sitting down all day long in chairs. The latest health studies show that sitting down for hours at a time can cut your life expectancy. Stand more when working. If you're on the phone, take the call standing up and walk around.

**Core Discipline #3: Emotional Health**

As we discussed in the Black Hole chapter, a rough patch in your life can kick you to the curb emotionally. People with emotional trauma or difficulties—depression, anxiety, addiction, relationship issues, or others—often try to bury themselves in work or some other outlet in order to ignore the problems they are feeling deep inside. But this masking will only last so long before that problem starts to work its way into other parts of your life.

Establishing self-reflection and creating self-awareness equals more sustainable emotional health. You have to ask yourself tough questions and you have to be honest with yourself about where you are. Use the detachment skill that you are learning for critical thinking to take a step back and rationally consider the factors that compose your emotional health. When you feel emotion, figure out what it is and assign it a label, so that when it surges up and becomes overwhelming, you will recognize it for what it is. Once you recognize it, see if you can figure out what triggered it. Do you see any patterns in your emotional triggers? Can you change your circumstances to avoid these triggers?

You have to also learn to ask other people to help you maintain your emotional health. You have to be transparent to be open to receiving assistance. Some of us have so many boundaries, so many layers, that people don't really know who we are. We have secret fears, doubts, insecurities, and hurts from the past. We hide those behind shields so people can't see the true us. Let down some of those shields. Let people in. Let other people help you strengthen your emotional health. When you talk about the things that are scary to talk about, and you learn that the people who love you will still love you despite your fears, then those fears start to lose their power over you.

## Core Discipline #4 Learning how to Maximize and Prioritize your Time

*UNTIL WE CAN MANAGE TIME, WE CAN MANAGE NOTHING ELSE.*

—*Peter Drucker*

Time can be your best friend or your worst enemy.

Wherever your heart is, that's where you'll spend your time. That's why it's so important to invest your time in doing something that you really love, because otherwise, you can't wait to leave it and move onto something more fun, like going to the dentist, or taking out the garbage! For instance, accountants derive great pleasure from making spreadsheets and making sure all the numbers add up. Copyeditors make sure that grammar rules are adhered to on each and every line. Nurses live for making their patients' lives easier and more comfortable. Do I want to be a numbers guy, copyeditor, or nurse? No, but I admire people who follow their passion to make the world a healthier, more orderly place. I love to speak and motivate people, whereas a lot of people would rather face a firing squad than speak in front of a group of people.

One of the biggest time wasters is staying stuck in the past while trying to figure out your future. So if your heart has not left the locker room, you're going to waste your time thinking about how you're going to get back. Don't get caught in that trap.

A difficult thing for an ex-athlete whose time was regimented during the season is to know how to set priorities. You'll end up putting things that are not important in front of the things that are. For instance, a woman I know who is a mother of two little boys used to shop at Trader Joe's three times a week for her groceries when she was a stay-at-home mom. Now she has a very busy part-time job, and said, "I realized it's not necessary to shop at Trader Joe's three times a week anymore—I can live just going there once a week." Often, we make work for ourselves when we are not busy, and then discover when truly busy with other work that we no longer need to do things the way we used to.

> *PEOPLE OFTEN COMPLAIN ABOUT LACK OF TIME WHEN THE LACK OF DIRECTION IS THE REAL PROBLEM.*
>
> —*Zig Ziglar*

Everything that you try to manage requires time. So learn what it is that you can manage, and what is outside your ability to influence.

Early in my transition, I thought that everything that I was involved in required the same amount of effort and time, which didn't allow me to prioritize what required my passion. I was a meeting fool. I was just meeting to meet, networking like crazy. But a lot of the meetings weren't productive. I was searching for something to fill the hole where football used to be, to recreate something I had in the past, instead of searching for something that would allow me to be attached in a new and meaningful way. I was afraid I was going to miss something, instead of trusting and having faith in my own abilities. I was hoping that if I threw myself into every possible thing, some opportunity would just appear.

I had to learn what was bearing fruit for me and my family in order to see where I was spending my time wisely. So eventually I stopped going to every networking meeting that was available, and learned where to spend my most valuable time. It started to pay off when I became more intentional in this area.

If you are in transition and haven't found a new role yet, there's everything right with allowing yourself time to try new things, network, and create new relationships. Build up your resume. Learn some new skills. The more time you spend doing this, if you are self-reflective and analytical, you will start to see that some of the things you're doing are more fulfilling than others. Some activities leave you feeling satisfied and inspired, while others leave you feeling drained and discouraged. Keep a journal, and make notes about how you feel after you do certain things. Soon enough, patterns will emerge, and you may be able to follow them to the next stage of your life.

At the end of the day, God is only giving you time to do things in, and if you you're wasting your time, then you're wasting the gift that He's given you. Besides, if you are trying to inspire your children to be go-getters, they can't see you sitting around all day long and not going anywhere. Show them what it means to find your purpose—and don't worry if it's hard. They don't need to see everything coming easily to you; they need to see you working to make your life something you're proud of.

What you have done with your time on earth has made you who you are today. Your past has shaped who you are; what you do now will determine who you become.

## Core Discipline #5: Building New Attachments

When you're an athlete, you feel comfortable in the locker room, on the field, on the ice, or on the court. It feels like a second home to you, and your team feels like a second family. You become attached to those places and people. But now it's not your second home anymore, and you need to build a new environment.

Be careful of bringing your old mind-set into a new land. New land = fresh start. Invest in a setting where you feel inspired and purposeful every day. Create an inspiring mood around your office space so that you feel like you are meant to be there and proud to show it off. You want to own your space. You want to bring a level of pride to what you're doing. Remember all those Coins you collected in Chapter Three? Bring reminders of them into your work space. Decorate with pictures that bring you back to a place of being proud, and leave room to add to your new environment. I have my two degrees hanging in my office, certificates of courses that I completed, and a game ball that I was awarded. I have a picture of my daughter from when she was small, and artwork that she did that reminds me of family. I even have a certificate that my mom received before she retired that praised her work ethic, to remind me of how hard she worked to raise my siblings and me. My office shelves are lined with books, motivational tapes, and music that inspires me. Create a space that you're proud of and one that brings you joy.

As you explore different ways to make your time meaningful, you may find new activities or causes that will inspire attachment. A new exercise class may challenge your body in new ways, and lead you to try other new physical outlets. Reading to school kids or volunteering with a nonprofit organization whose mission has meaning to you could become a regular part of your routine, and could even lead you to discover career possibilities you hadn't considered. And as you find more ways to connect with your community, you will probably meet new people you connect with, too—more opportunities to build attachment.

One high school teacher I know made sure that his students never sat in the same desk day after day. He didn't want them to ever see life from the same perspective because he felt they would become complacent in seeing the same view day after day. Mix up your vantage points—don't always go to the same restaurants, ordering the same thing, seeing the same people. You don't want your world to get small. You want it to expand. I'm not saying that it's bad to see the same people, but don't be afraid to venture out. You are not alone, even though you might feel like it at times.

### Don't Gamble with Social Media

We all know how much fun social media can be on a personal level, but from a professional perspective, social networking has really become a must. If you are looking for a new job, seeking to change professions, or just want keep up with your business, trends, or industry, every headhunter, recruiter, and professional coach will advise you to get connected online, through LinkedIn, Facebook, Twitter, and other social media platforms.

What I urge you to keep at the forefront of your mind every single time you send a text or post anything on any online forum is this: nothing you text or put online is ever guaranteed to be private. You can ruin your reputation in a matter of seconds with the stroke of an ill-advised character, image, or word. If it appears on someone's phone screen, all they have to do is take a screen shot and it's preserved forever. Think it can't happen to you? I have seen kids lose scholarships and adults lose jobs for texting, sexting, YouTubing, and making thoughtless, cruel, incriminating, or just plain stupid posts on social media. If you think no one is watching you but your best buddies, you're wrong.

Just as you should in real life, put your best self forward online, and never post anything that you wouldn't want your grandmother, your child, or a potential employer to see.

**Core Discipline #6: Learning How to Trust and Be Accountable**

Do not expect that the old way of thinking that served you well in your past life will continue to work in every environment.

Trust is about learning how to discern a situation and evaluate it. You have to treat every situation and opportunity as its own entity. If you carry distrust forward with you from a bad past experience, you will miss out on the incredible value of putting faith in a trustworthy person. Every situation is unique. Every person deserves the chance to prove themselves worthy of your trust.

I had to learn to do that. I would think, *Everybody on the NFL team acts the same*, but that wasn't true. I grew up seeing the KKK on the corner, but if I branded every white person as a violent racist, I would have stayed stuck. I have to judge every new person I meet through the process of what I learn when I sit down with them. You can't allow a bad experience to overwhelm your belief system.

Back in Chapter Seven I discussed building a new team with a mentor, and all types of diverse friends and colleagues. These people will help keep you focused and accountable. Unless you want to fail, surround yourself with people who will hold you accountable! All successful people are accountable to someone. Every coach has a coach and usually every mentor has a mentor.

When I meet with a client, the first thing we do is take an assessment and identify what it is that she or he wants to accomplish, and then identify the things that are keeping them from doing it. Then it's time to make a list: how do I counter the things that are hindering me in getting what I want? Is it trust? Is it accountability? Is it not having the right team members?

**Core Discipline #8: Adjusting to a New Environment**

A lot of former players I know can't get over being in a new hierarchy of authority. If you're used to being a star player, you expect to be looked up to. But those star players need to remember where they are. I've been in meetings with other players, and had to remind them, "Hey it's not the locker room. You're not in control of this meeting right now. Be careful of bringing the wrong mentality and expectations into a meeting; it will be important to know your role in order to play it with excellence. You can't steamroll over everybody now. You can't make every place where you were.

One of my friends hired some publicists to help promote his book. These women used to work for a large publishing company, and had gone out on their own, utilizing the skills that they learned on the job to bring success to indie authors. My friend was used to getting feedback at all times of day from his employees and colleagues, and these women were used to giving monthly reports. When asked to give more updates faster, the publicists bristled at the thought, thinking that if the status quo was good enough for their old company, it was good enough for this individual. As a result, my friend was frustrated, and didn't get the service he wanted. And the publicists didn't get any referrals because of their refusal to adapt to their new marketplace.

You can't make the new place the same as the old one. See where you are now and not where you were.

It's OK not to say something in a meeting. It's easy to think you're going to miss your moment if you've always been in front. Humble yourself and sit at the foot of people who have been in this position for a while, knowing your ambitions are still alive and well. Watch, learn, and play a part once you have taken the time to see where you fit in.

## UNDERSTANDING THE IMPORTANCE OF IMAGE

When I was a professional football player, I used to love to travel in comfortable clothes: jogging pants, a T-shirt, a baseball hat, and running shoes. But when I started my own company, I had to change and realize that now I'm supporting my new image. I could no longer count on the NFL's reputation to precede me as a football player. (Note: teams are required to travel to games in a blazer and tie.) Now that I was representing Wheeler Enterprises, I needed to wear slacks, a dress shirt or polo shirt, or even a tie on the plane, just so I would present the right image. If you go into the NFL office, every man there is wearing a tie and sports coat, and all the women are in suits or work dresses. I now have to arrange for all my travel plans, meals, find places to work out. Booking everything makes me appreciate even more what I had back as a player, but now I appreciate the freedom that I have to do what I want and when I want.

When you played a sport, you wore a uniform with pride. But when ex-athletes show up in athletic gear to business meetings? Oh, no. You must dress the part of the role you want to play in your own life.

I have a friend right now: everywhere he goes, he thinks it's OK to wear jeans, tennis shoes, and a nylon shirt hanging out over his pants. He's still playing the role of the athlete, even though he's in another stage of his life.

Play the part that's required. You need a helmet to play football; you need spikes to run track; you need business attire to conduct business. It doesn't matter if you don't like it; get out of your own prideful way. You're going to have people tell you not to worry about what you wear, that it's what's in your head that matters. But people will judge you before you open your mouth and if you don't believe me, pay attention to it more closely next time, and you be the judge.

What does a life uniform look like for you now? Ask your mentors or people on your team for advice going into every meeting—what is appropriate to wear there? Although nobody is asking you to get a Savile Row tailored suit or dress, you do need to invest in yourself for the next role you have to play. If you can't spend the time investing in you, why should anyone else waste their time?

**Journal:**

Identify two disciplines from the chapter that you need to implement in your transition.

_____

_____

_____

_____

_____

_____

_____

_____

Why is creating a new environment important to you? What does it look like?

_____

_____

_____

_____

_____

_____

_____

_____

Are you making yourself available to new opportunities?

_____

_____

_____

_____

_____

_____

# PART FOUR:

## SHOW ME THE MONEY

People ask me the same question over and over: "How do professional athletes go broke so quickly after making millions?" First, most professional athletes do not make millions. Second, how do you know that most professional athletes go broke without knowing the athletes themselves?

Eugene Robinson's mentor, David Brown, opened Eugene's eyes to financial responsibility very early in his NFL career:

*One day, Dave, came over to my apartment and asked me and my wife a probing question: "What are you doing with your money, Rookie?"*

*That threw me. "Man, Dave! That's a bit personal. I'm not sure."*

*"I know you don't know, Rook, so let me give you a plan. Gene, when you're done playing, I don't want you to be among the casualties who has nothing to show for their time in the NFL. Even though you are making the minimum [that was $65,000 in 1985], if you save and keep your cost of living at a modest level, you can win." He went on to tell me that God wants me to owe no man anything but love, so being debt-free was the only option. He told me to own everything, don't pay a mortgage if possible, and definitely own your cars. He told me to keep my cost of living at a level that is comfortable and let your salary rise. He told me that God expects me to tithe 10 percent to the church (God loves a cheerful giver) and to pay my taxes ("Give to Caesar what belongs to Caesar."). "Rook, resist the urge of extravagances, be prudent, pay your bills and save for your kids' and grandkids' future." I did not even have any kids at the time.*

*This was sound advice from a man who walked the very same model he was proposing to me, and I took it. My final season ended in 2000 with the Carolina Panthers. My wife and I were able to put our two kids through private school and college. We now own two homes, my personal residence and a home I bought for my mom. We own our cars and I've been able to put money away for the future. It's been 14 years since I retired, and we are not among the many who are bankrupt and divorced when they exited the NFL. We have investments that pay us an annual salary. I have funds (Praise God!) for retirement. I work as a broadcaster and high school coach.*

*I didn't know how long football would last and I wanted to be prepared in case I was cut, waived, fired, injured, or abruptly OUT! I was not attracted to the allure of the sensational. My home life was stable; I have a wonderful supportive and loving wife and two awesome kids, now grown. I am ordinary man afforded a golden opportunity, and I hope I made the best of it.*

Eugene was very fortunate to have such solid guidance from a trusted adviser. But even without a mentor, you can make a financial plan that will serve you well throughout your life.

I have built a great relationship with Lincoln Financial and they have helped to provide information for this chapter of my book—full of great advice about establishing financial goals and protecting you, your family, and your money.

Please do not allow the fear of not being financially astute to hinder you from asking questions about finances. You may think it's embarrassing not to know something, but it would be far more embarrassing, and far more devastating, to end up in bankruptcy because you were afraid to ask questions.

**Chapter Ten:**

## DEVELOPING A FINANCIAL
## GAME PLAN FOR LIFE
*by Pete Mastrantuono, Lincoln Financial*

*"Would you tell me, please, which way I ought to walk from
here?"*

*"That depends a good deal on where you want to get to,"
said the Cat.*

*"I don't much care where—" said Alice.*

*"Then it doesn't matter which way you walk," said the Cat.*

*—Lewis Carroll, Alice's Adventures In Wonderland*

If you don't have a direction in life, then it really doesn't matter
much which road you take. The value of having defined goals is
that you set a destination of your choosing, and plan the path to get
you there.

If you are old enough to read this book, you are old enough to
understand how to be fiscally responsible. Just as a team develops
a game plan, or an athlete creates goals for the season, you need
to develop a game plan for your future. In your financial life, that
game plan is about creating a financial plan that sets goals, assesses
your current financial state, and implements a course of action to
reach your goals. A financial plan should be reviewed periodically,

typically on an annual basis, or whenever you are facing a major life change.

Depending on what stage of life you're in, a financial plan can be simple. But with age and more money comes greater complexity. Whatever your situation, it's important that you begin with a plan because, as Benjamin Franklin put it, "by failing to prepare, you are preparing to fail." In other words, "failing to plan is planning to fail."

## Budgeting and Cash Flow Planning

Setting goals can sometimes be overwhelming. Your goals may include saving for a house, a car, a wedding, or even your retirement. Each individual goal might require funds that seem to be well beyond the reach of your income. Don't let this discourage you. Some of these goals are many years away, and, as you'll learn later, young savers have the distinct advantage of time and the power of compounding interest to help meet these goals.

Let's first discuss how to lay the foundation for reaching your financial goals. It begins with a commitment to budgeting and cash flow planning.

The fewer resources you have, the more efficient you need to become with them. This requires that you understand how you spend each dollar you earn. To get started, begin recording every purchase you make for the next month, right down to the morning coffee you buy on the way to work. Gather your monthly bills. Don't forget to include the bills that may come quarterly or annually, like car insurance. This can be a tedious exercise, but most people are surprised by how much money they spend on things that are not very important to them, or provide only temporary satisfaction.

Computer programs like Quicken make it very easy to import information from your bank and credit cards, and will help you track your income and expenses in great detail. Downloading one of the many good phone apps for tracking expenses might help you with day-to-day budget tracking. An app allows you to record your spending immediately, saving you from having to keep receipts or forgetting about some purchases.

When the month has ended, begin putting together a snapshot of your spending by category. Create your own categories—some general ones may include food, housing, utilities, car, clothing, hobbies, entertainment, charity, etc.

Now it's time to review your spending habits. What do you see? Are you surprised by how much you've spent on spontaneous purchases of clothing? Did even small things, like the $3 morning cup of coffee, add up? Did you realize the number of times you eat out in a month?

You may think that such spending can't possibly be meaningful, but consider this example: The $90 per month you identify as unnecessary spending, if saved, can grow to over $15,500 in 10 years, assuming a rate of return of just 7 percent.

At the core of this spending review is that you are the one who gets to make the choices about your spending habits and set your priorities. No one is suggesting that you eliminate the $3 morning coffee if it provides you with some psychic reward or irreplaceable convenience, but there may be other things you are spending money on that you are comfortable reducing.

Cash flow planning and budgeting is really an exercise in self-empowerment. It puts you in control to decide for yourself what your hierarchy of needs is, so that you can apply your resources to the things that are most important to you.

### The Offensive Playbook

Before we begin discussing how to build your wealth, let's spend a little time talking about debt. Thanks to college costs, many young Americans begin their adult lives burdened with a considerable amount of debt. This debt can be a significant drag on wealth accumulation.

The first strategy for reducing debt is to try to avoid it in the first place.

For instance, for those thinking about college, if attending a four-year college will mean taking on substantial debt, consider attending a less expensive community college for the first two years. You will be still able to receive a degree from the four-year school of your choice, but at less cost. Consider working while in school. It may mean a greater personal challenge and less time for socializing, but you will be happy that you did so in your post-graduation years.

If you want to get a master's degree, think about going to work for an employer that offers a tuition reimbursement benefit that will help fund the cost of obtaining this degree. It may take longer to earn that degree, but it will be a much more valuable one when it's attached to the real world experience you gained.

Consider paying a bit extra each month on your schedule of payments for monthly bills like a mortgage or car payments. You will retire your debt earlier, and save possibly thousands of dollars in future interest charges.

Not all debt is bad, and not all debt is avoidable, but the buildup of too much debt will be a drag on your wealth accumulation goals. Carry this reluctance to take on debt into your future years. Credit card debt is one of the more destructive forms of debt since it so often used for purchases of fleeting value and short life. It can become particularly insidious when you only pay the minimum amount due each month, leading to accumulating balances and ever-increasing interest charges.

### Establishing An Emergency Fund

Most financial planners agree that you should build an emergency fund equal to 3-6 months of living expenses. This emergency fund will serve two purposes.

1. It can help pay for large, unexpected expenses that can't be managed by your paycheck, for instance: car repairs or replacing a broken appliance; and
2. It will help you be prepared in the event of a job loss. It is no secret that economic uncertainties have led to layoffs and

extended job search times. Having the financial safety net of an emergency fund will not only help you through the difficulties of a job loss, but it also helps you to be more discriminating in accepting your next job. With the ability to meet current living expenses, you won't be forced to take the first available job because you need the money. The emergency fund will give you more time to find a job that better fits with your career aspirations.

To establish your emergency fund, considering putting aside a set amount each paycheck into a bank account of your choice until you've reached the desired level of emergency savings. Only you can decide how much you can put away, but a regular, disciplined practice of setting aside money will eventually get you there.

With an emergency fund in place and a commitment to budgeting, you need to determine your personal financial goals and how much you need to save for them. Your goals and your path to realizing them are as individual as your fingerprint. You may have multiple long-term goals that you wish to save for simultaneously (e.g., a child's college education and retirement), or sequentially (e.g., first a down payment on a house, then retirement).

Once you've identified what your goals are, you will need to determine how much you need to save to accumulate the funds required. Whether your goal is retirement or a house, there are plenty of tools to help you ascertain the level of monthly savings required to reach your desired savings goal. Alternatively, you may choose to work with a financial professional to calculate your savings needs.

Do not get discouraged if you cannot presently meet the indicated savings requirements. Getting started is more important than having enough to save. Over time, your career will progress and income will increase so the ending to your story is never fully written in the first few chapters.

Once you've identified your goals and gained an understanding of a realistic savings program, you will then be faced with how to best make your money work for you to achieve your financial objectives. With that, let's begin reviewing some important principles and guidelines for building your wealth.

## The Basic Principles of Investing

In any sport, success is all about mastering the fundamentals and executing them well. Growing your wealth starts with several fundamental principles. Executing them will be key to your success.

### Start Early

This principle reflects several basic truths. The first is that by starting early, you can benefit from the power of compounding, which Albert Einstein once called, "The most powerful force in the universe." The power of compounding refers to the accumulation of earnings generated on previous earnings—the longer the period, the more powerful its effect.

To illustrate this, let's use the example of two investors, Damon and Allison, both age 25.

- Damon decides to begin investing early. He begins immediately to save $2,000 per year for the next ten years, or until he is 35 years old, at which point he stops saving any new money.
- Allison, on the other hand, waits until she is 35 years old and begins to invest $2,000 for the next 20 years, until she reaches the age of 55.
- During this 30-year period (from age 25 to age 55), Damon has saved a total of $20,000, while Allison has put away $40,000. Assuming that both Damon and Allison received the same 7 % average annual rate of return, can you guess who has more money by age 55?
- It turns out that Damon's $20,000 in savings grew to $106,931, while Allison's $40,000 in savings grew to just $81,991! How is that Allison saved twice as much as Damon and ended up with almost $25,000 less in savings? Because

Damon saved his money earlier, there was more time for his money to generate earnings. As he earned, the earnings were added to his base amount, so the amount of money he was earning interest on grew, thus generating more interest. Ten more years of this ended up adding more to his bottom line than he had saved in the first place!

- Let's also not overlook the fact that $20,000 grew to over $100,000 thanks to all those earnings on previous earnings. Amazing!

*Pay Yourself First*

This concept suggests that you think of your financial goals as another financial obligation that needs to be paid off. Make this your most important obligation. As we've emphasized, you can't expect to have all the resources to fund your goals, but you should carve out an amount to save prior to any spending. Much like taxes deducted from your paycheck represent income that you can't spend, do the same for savings. Pick an amount to save and "pay yourself first." The money leftover after taxes and savings will be what you can spend to meet your bills and other living expenses. You will quickly find that you won't miss what you don't have.

*Diversify, Diversify, Diversify*

We've all heard the saying, "Don't put all your eggs in one basket." This is never truer than with investing. Investments can go through cycles of being in style. Remember the dot-com boom and when everybody was buying fixer-upper houses to turn over for huge profits? The challenge for investors is that you can never be certain when real estate or technology stocks will be in favor or out of favor, or for how long.

So it's best to diversify across a broad spectrum of asset classes that includes large and small company stocks, US and international companies, and bonds. This diversification should be structured to meet your investment objectives and be in line with your tolerance for risk.

Mutual funds provide an ideal way to save small amounts of money and achieve immediate diversification.

### Risk and Return are Always Linked

There is no such thing as high returns with low risk. Never! *If it's too good to be true, then it probably is* is wise advice.

The smartest thing you can do when you hear claims about the potential for outsized returns with little to no risk is to walk away. It will be a decision that will save you a lot of money over your lifetime.

The reason why a low-risk / high-return investment is not possible is found in the nature of how markets work. If an investment did exist that showed low risk and high return, investors would rapidly move in, driving up the price and reducing its potential for future gains, quickly turning this idea into a low-return, low-risk opportunity.

The idea that you can obtain high returns with little risk requires that you believe that the thousands of professional investors who spend their entire working days looking for attractive investment opportunities (along with millions of individual investors) would fail to find this "surefire" idea. The widespread nature of information in our modern age makes this extremely unlikely.

### Match Investments to Time Horizon of Goals

Each of your goals has its own time frame. For instance, your goal to build savings for a down payment on a car in six months is a goal with a short-term time horizon. For that goal, you'll want to place your savings in something with little downside risk, such as bank deposits or money market funds. The reason you want to avoid investments that have short-term volatility (such as stocks) is that you could incur losses at the moment you need the money, impacting your ability to meet your goal.

Saving for your retirement is a goal with a long-term time horizon. As such, you'll want to invest in a broadly diversified portfolio comprised predominantly of stocks, since they have historically provided growth over longer time periods. Since you will not need to use your retirement savings in the near-term, the short-term volatility of stocks is a risk that you can weather in order to benefit from their long-term capital appreciation potential.

*Time in the Market, Not Timing the Market*

Many individuals imagine that they can make smart invest-ment choices and then move in and out of the market as it moves through its cycles of ups and downs. Few individuals can do that consistently. Most harm themselves by trying to outsmart the market. Let's see what happens to real investors when they seek to time the markets.

In its 2011 annual report on investor behavior, Dalbar, a leading financial services research firm, found that over the 20-year period ending 2010, that investor returns in US stock mutual funds averaged an annual return of 3.27%, significantly lagging the 9.14% average annual return of the S&P 500, a broad measure of the stock market. The primary reason for this gap was due to investor deci-sions to exit and enter the markets (i.e., timing the market).

A recent analysis by Putnam Investments, a large investment manager, illustrates why timing the market is so difficult. In the period from 12/31/97 to 12/31/12, if you stayed fully invested in the stock market your average annual return would have been 5.8%. If you missed just ten of the best performing days during these 15 years, your return would have fallen to 1.17%. If you missed the best 20 days, you would have lost money.

The lesson here is that market returns can occur at any time, and frequently when we least expect it. By trying to time the market, you increase your chances of not being in the market to profit from its best days.

*Avoid Fads*

As you begin your investing journey, you will see articles and stories about how some mutual fund or company is out-returning similar investments; those stories may even highlight individuals who have reaped enormous gains. These stories may make you want a piece of that action. Bad idea.

Investment crazes have been around as long as individuals have had money to invest. During a craze a point is reached where prices cease to make any economic sense, and where continued price increases rely on "the greater fool theory" (i.e., there are more fools left out there to pay overinflated prices). Eventually you run out of fools (there is a limited supply of them despite indications otherwise) and when new investors become scarce, prices will fall. Investment crazes often end with a loud and painful crash.

### Watch Fees, Expenses, and Taxes

Generally speaking, the markets are very efficient, which is to say that all the information is well known and distributed broadly, making the value of assets fairly priced—usually. (The markets have been known to become very inefficient, e.g., the Flash Crash of May 6, 2010, a day during which the stock market plummeted 5-6% in a matter of minutes, and then recovered almost as quickly.)

Because the markets are mostly efficient, most of time, it is very difficult to outperform the market. Some money managers have succeeded. Fewer have done it consistently. In view of this, you will want to be careful about the fees and expenses you pay to someone or to a mutual fund to manage your money. Excessive fees will work against performance results and, over an extended period of time, will stunt your wealth accumulation.

Taxes can be a significant drain on investment performance as well. You can reduce their impact by investing in tax-deferred accounts such as IRAs or 401(k)s, or by limiting the level of buying and selling of investments, which results in owing taxes on any investment profits.

### Be Careful About Losses

The markets are volatile and reacting to every cough or sniffle in the stock market will lead you away from your goals. As with much of life, general rules tend to generally work well, but there are exceptions.

Regardless of your intelligence or investment experience, you will make mistakes and they will result in losses—get used to it; losses are part of the landscape of investing. At times you will need to cut your losses. Losses can cause substantial harm to your wealth accumulation. For instance, if you lose 25% on a particular investment, how much do you think you need to recover to get back to your original value? If you said 34%, you'd be correct. Here's the explanation: If, for example, you have $10,000 invested and it loses 25%, it will now be worth $7,500. In order for your investment to get back to its original value, it will need to increase by 34% ($7,500 X 1.34 = $10,050). Lose 50% and you need a 100% return to get back to even. You can readily see how difficult it is to recover from large losses.

To avoid large losses, you should have a discipline for selling investments by setting your "sell" price at the time you make the investment. That should help you from holding onto a bad investment in the hopes it will turn around. One way to do this is via a "stop loss" order. Whether you invest through a financial advisor or on your own, you are able to instruct your broker (or indicate on the buy transaction, if you are trading on your own) that you want to place a "stop loss" order in which you indicate the price at which you want to sell it automatically.

### Participate in Your Employer's 401(k)

The best place to begin to save for retirement is by participating in your employer's 401(k) plan. There are several benefits of participation.

1. Your contributions to the plan are pre-tax. That means the money you save is not subject to the taxes you see withheld from your gross pay. Because of this, saving in a 401(k) plan has less of an impact on your take-home pay than you think. An example will help illustrate this. Let's assume you want to save $100 per month in your 401(k). You might think that means that you will be taking home $100 less per month. In

fact, your take-home pay will only be reduced by $85, assuming you are subject to a 15% tax rate. This is because the $100 you save means that you won't pay $15 in tax on that amount so it becomes part of your take home pay.

2. Your investments grow tax-deferred, i.e., investment earnings are not reduced by taxes until they are withdrawn. This allows your savings to grow faster and larger. It's like a turbo charge to the power of compounding, because you'll have more earnings compounding than if you saved outside of a 401(k) plan where your earnings would be reduced by taxes.

3. Many employers match their employees' contributions. For example, if you make $40,000 per year and contribute 5% to the 401(k), you will be saving $2,000 a year. If your employer matches your contribution up to say, 3% of your salary, your employer will contribute $1,200 to your account! When an employer matches contributions, not participating in your employer's 401(k) plan is like giving a part of your salary away—not the best way to grow your wealth.

## Success Lies not in Our Stars, but in Ourselves

We like to imagine that investing is some rational exercise in which we coolly assess the facts and make calculated decisions, but it's not—even for professionals.

The future is unknowable and when it involves our money, it is unavoidable that emotions will be heightened. Our emotions are not the only thing that works against us. We are also saddled with any number of innate biases that work against smart decision-making.

## Mastering Your Emotions and Biases

Fidelity Investments, one of the largest money managers in the world and a leading provider of 401(k) services to small and large companies across the United States, published a study that analyzed the investment decisions of their 401(k) account holders in the wake of the market collapse in 2008.

The study found that individuals who reduced stock holdings in their 401(k) to 0% during the trough of the stock market (October 1, 2008—March 31, 2009) experienced a 2% return on their assets by June 30, 2011. Those who reduced their stock holdings, but not entirely, averaged 25% returns. However, those who did nothing—they kept all their stock holdings during the worst of the market—experienced a 50% return on their portfolio as of June 30, 2011.

This illustration is not meant to diminish or criticize these folks. Unquestionably, it is very scary to see your life savings fall by 30 or 40%. The intention of this illustration is to emphasize how important rational decision-making is to your investment success. With that, let's review some tips to consider.

### Fear and Greed—Control the Passions

Fear and greed are powerful emotions that drive not just personal decision-making, but collectively can create the sort of mania in the markets that drive prices to diverge from all reasonable levels.

In a bull (good) market, greed can become a consuming emotion in which we discard reason and common sense in the belief that prices will go higher still and we'll get ever richer. Frequently, we rationalize this irrational thinking by convincing ourselves that *this time it's different*. The "dot-com bubble" is a perfect example of this. Despite extraordinary valuations, investors during the period 1997-2000 committed more and more money to internet stocks. Companies with no products or sales were valued more than some companies with established brands and consistent profitability. Investors had convinced themselves that somehow internet stocks had to be viewed differently than how stocks historically were evaluated. Investor greed clouded good judgment, and on March 10, 2000 the NASDAQ Index (a technology-dominated index) peaked at 5132.52. By the end of the year, it had fallen to 2471, an over 50% decline in value. It continued to fall, reaching a low of 1173, a 77% loss in value. Over thirteen years later, the NASDAQ Index remains below the internet-driven craze high it reached in March 2000.

During a bear (bad) market or a market crash, the fear of losing money can result in a "flight" impulse thanks to our primal instinct to run from danger. This fear can lead us to sell investments at precisely the worst time. In fact, history proves time and again that the best time to invest is when pessimism reigns, for that is the seed for the next bull market.

The best weapon against these powerful emotions is to have a plan. A plan is your north star that keeps you on your path to success and from succumbing to these two destructive emotions.

Your financial plan acts just like a game plan in sports. A game plan helps identify your team's strength and weaknesses, as well as your opponent's. From that emerges a strategy that leads to victory. As any athlete knows, a game never goes precisely according to plan, but the plan is never abandoned at the first setback or surprise. Successful coaches and players don't panic in the face of adversity, and they don't grow overconfident if early events favor them. They stick to the plan, because they know it remains their best path to achieving success. Same with a financial plan: you've plotted a path to success with an understanding of your objectives and risk tolerance. Whether it is a sharp decline in the market or sharply rising prices, your financial plan is a reminder of how success will be achieved. Like a game plan, it will keep you from desperation if you fall behind early, or from overconfidence if the markets provide an early lead.

### Overconfidence—Don't Commit the Sin of Thinking You're Smarter

Research repeatedly tells us that individually we think we're better and smarter than most people. For instance, in surveys, drivers nearly always rate their driving abilities above the majority of drivers when, of course, the majority of drivers cannot be better than the majority of drivers.

Confidence is not necessarily a bad thing. It can work wonders in competitive sports and in the business world. But *over*confidence can blind us to certain things. In sports, it might lead us not to train hard enough for an opponent. In investing, overconfidence can lead to mistakes as well.

Sometimes overconfidence arises from what is called "confirmation bias." Confirmation bias is the tendency to listen to only the news or facts that support our conclusions or beliefs. Many people do not like hearing opinions or facts that challenge their beliefs. This bias is often why conservative-leaning individuals tend to watch or read conservative-oriented media, and liberal-leaning individuals gravitate to more liberal-oriented media. People like to hear that which confirms their beliefs.

This bias can lead to expensive mistakes. To avoid this error, make sure you seek out opinions that run counter to your investment thesis. Remain open-minded about the case against your idea or position. It takes a certain amount of personal strength, indeed self-confidence, to welcome opposing ideas, but it will serve you well. Using your broker (human or online), ask for all research they may have on a company or market sector that you think is especially attractive. Search the internet to uncover different viewpoints about the company's or sector's prospects. Ask yourself, "What developments or events can upend an anticipated outcome?"

We also suffer from a "home bias." You may have heard the expression, "invest in what you know." While it is important that you know what you're investing in, it can be problematic if you concentrate too much of your portfolio in companies that you know or are close to you.

A common mistake people make is to invest a disproportionate share of their savings in their employer's stock. Remember, it's not only your savings that are dependent on the company, but so too is your current income. History is replete with stories of individuals' wealth evaporating as a consequence of the business difficulties of their employer. Enron and WorldCom are a couple of the more spectacular and tragic examples.

Learn to embrace your mistakes; learning from them will be one of your greatest investments! The earlier in life you do this, the fewer mistakes you'll make later in life when you have more money and the consequences of those mistakes are far more expensive.

It might help to keep an investing diary to record your deci-sions so that you won't selectively forget your mistakes. Better still, design a paper portfolio and make investment decisions for prac-tice. Consider it a "portfolio fantasy league." This practice portfolio will help you learn important lessons at no cost!

### Predicting the Markets

Humans have an innate desire to recognize patterns and apply these patterns to predicting the future. Our inclination to predict events causes us to place too much weight on previous events, in the belief that they will influence future outcomes. This is called "positive expectation bias." One common example of this is flipping a penny seven times and each time it comes up "heads." Despite the trend of "heads," the odds of the next toss coming up "tails" is still 50%, the same odds as each previous flip.

Another destructive bias is "negativity bias." This is our bias to place more emphasis on bad news than good news. Television has made a business out of this. If you were to ask most people if crime, violence, and war have increased or decreased, they would likely say they've increased. As Steven Pinker describes in his book, *The Better Angels of Our Nature: Why Violence Has Declined*, violence and injustice have actually decreased over time. This negativity bias runs the risk of dwelling on negative news at the expense of good news.

In the investment world, this means we may focus on news that may adversely affect the markets and discount the good news that might propel the market higher. It's the sort of bias that keeps us from investing when it might in fact be the best time to do so.

Implement a disciplined investment plan like a monthly peri-odic investment program. Then, just stick with the basic principles we outlined earlier.

### Current Moment Bias

Very often we act like the future may never come. Sadly, we seem wired to prefer pleasure in the current moment and to put off the pain for later. We prefer the pleasure of a nice car or expensive night out now and ignore the pain of not having sufficient savings tomorrow. Don't allow the current moment bias to delay that which you should be doing today.

Whatever your goals, you may find that personal contentment is the best measure of your wealth, and your happiness.

## The Defensive Playbook

As in sports, victory is about having a defensive game plan along with an offensive game plan. We can score all we like, but if we have no way of stopping the opposition, victory will always be in doubt. The sports cliché that "defense wins championships" may be a suspect truism in modern sports, but to quote Warren Sapp, "defense gives you a chance."

In your financial life, you want to think about a strong defense against the financial setbacks that can upend your efforts to build wealth. Life is risky. Much like wearing a bike helmet or having a designated driver mitigates certain risks, you can take steps that reduce the financial risks you may face in your lifetime.

Financial risks may include the risk that your home burns down, or your car is totaled in an accident. Maybe you get ill and medical bills soar. You also face the risk of death or disability, which impacts the financial security of you and your loved ones.

The likelihood of many of these risks occurring is quite low, but their financial cost to you can be catastrophic. Imagine your house burning down and the financial loss that might entail. You would need to rebuild your home and still have to pay back the bank on the mortgage even though your house was destroyed. Plus, you'd have to find temporary housing and buy new furniture and appliances. Without insurance, most Americans would not be able to recover financially from this experience.

Let's take a closer look at several ways to protect yourself from common risks that can undermine building your wealth.

## Insuring Your Greatest Asset

*I'M NOT A BUSINESSMAN. I'M A BUSINESS, MAN*

—Jay-Z

Pop quiz: What is your single greatest asset? Did you say your car? Your home? Perhaps your current savings? Actually you would be wrong on all counts. Your single greatest asset is *you*. Nothing holds greater monetary value than your capacity to earn money for decades to come. For most individuals, it may not be until they are into their late fifties or sixties that other assets such as a home or 401(k) will be worth more than their future earnings potential.

Thus, the first, second, and third rule in your defensive playbook is to protect this most important asset. The primary dangers to your ability to earn future income are death and disability. Let's look at each separately.

*Life Insurance*

Your immediate question may be "What do I care about future income if I'm dead?" If you are single person with no kids, you would be right to think that it's not a concern of yours. However, early adulthood for many individuals involves the formation of new families; we get married and have children. Imagine yourself in a situation in which you contribute half the income in a two-income household with two young children. Now think about the financial challenges your surviving spouse would face should half the household income disappear due to your untimely death. Would your family be required to sell the house because the mortgage was reliant on contributing two incomes? How would daycare be paid on one income? How could your kids afford to go to college?

The purchase of life insurance helps to ensure the financial viability of your surviving family. Once you appreciate the need to protect your family's financial future, you'll need to make a couple of important decisions about the amount of coverage and type of coverage you'll want.

*Types of Life Insurance*

The two basic forms of life insurance are *term* and *permanent*. Term insurance receives its name because it covers you for a defined period of time (or term), e.g., fifteen years. Once the term expires, coverage is ended, and the premiums you paid over that period have no value to you.

Permanent insurance covers you for as long as you pay all the premiums. It combines the pure insurance coverage of a term policy with a form of savings, i.e., some portion of your premium is saved and invested inside the policy, which builds a cash value that you may access at some future point.

The payment of life insurance proceeds to the policy's beneficiary(ies) is tax-free. This is important to know when calculating your coverage needs. For instance, your annual income is reduced by federal and state taxes. Thus, you're not so much looking to replace your income dollar-for-dollar, but looking to calculate the after-tax income that will disappear. Another way to calculate your insurance needs is to identify annual living expenses (reduced by the surviving spouse's after-tax income) and factor in one-time expenses, such as your children's future college costs.

There are scores of reputable life insurance calculation tools that can help you begin determining the appropriate level of coverage. Begin your search for "life insurance calculators" and you will discover a rich set of choices. Try a couple of them to learn how much you might need.

*What type of coverage should you get?*

Because permanent insurance combines pure insurance coverage with savings, the premium cost for the same level of life insurance coverage will be substantially higher than the cost of term insurance.

Your life insurance coverage needs may never be higher than in your early adulthood (think of the coverage needed to pay for 15 or more years of living expenses and college costs 18 years from now!). Because of that, you will want the most coverage for your limited resources, which is what term insurance can provide.

The good news is, despite the high coverage amount you may need, term insurance has become increasingly cheaper, thanks to a lengthening lifespan and a competitive marketplace.

When examining term policies, you should consider policies that offer noncancelable and guaranteed-renewability provisions. This protects you from losing your policy based on the whims of the provider.

Remember, insurance is nothing more than a promise by one party (the insurance company) to pay out a future obligation to a second party (your survivors), so you want to make sure that you purchase a policy from a company that will be around to live up to that promise. Consider working only with highly rated insurance companies that have a history of making good on their claims. Thankfully, there are many candidates from which to choose.

### Disability Insurance

The chance of someone becoming disabled and being unable to work is far higher than dying. According to the Council for Disability Awareness, one in four of today's 20-year-olds will become disabled before they retire. This doesn't necessarily mean that they will become permanently disabled, but they may be disabled for a period of three months or more. Such extended periods of not earning an income can cause significant financial hardship. If you expect that Social Security Disability Insurance will cover such losses, it may be worth noting that 65 percent of all applications for such benefits were denied in 2012, and that 48 percent of SSDI recipients receive less than $1,000 per month.

There are two forms of disability coverage: short-term and long-term. Short-term disability is defined as a disability that renders you unable to do your job for a short, limited period of time (for example, up to 60 days, or 26 weeks). Long-term disability is defined as a disability that prevents you from performing your job for an extended period of time, measured in years.

Disability coverage may be made available through your

employer. The disability coverage that employers offer, and at what cost, will vary.

Disability insurance can be complex, much like life insurance, but, there are several important things to keep in mind.

Employer plans typically pay up to 60% of your income. This benefit, which may be taxable, may not be enough to meet your bills, which is why you may want to supplement any employer-based coverage with a personal policy. Supplemental policies may be purchased to cover up to generally 70–80% of your income.

When you pay the premiums on a personal disability policy, the benefit payments will be income tax free. This means that you will not need coverage equal to your current income since your take-home pay is always less than your gross salary.

Another important consideration is that there are waiting periods before disability payments begin. The waiting period is the time between the date of your disability and when actual payments begin. The longer this waiting period, the less expensive your disability coverage is. A longer waiting period will save you money, but it also means that you will need to live off your savings for a longer period of time. You are the best judge of this trade-off in lost dollars versus how much money you have in savings, and how much of this risk you are comfortable assuming.

In any event, you will want to coordinate the waiting period of your long-term disability coverage with your short-term disability benefits. For example, if your short-term disability covers you for 90 days, it would not be sensible to purchase a long-term disability policy with a 60-day waiting period. You would look to have at least a 90-day waiting period so that you can lower the cost on the long-term policy.

When you purchase disability insurance, the policy will define what constitutes an inability to work. Some policies will say "the inability to do any job or task"; others will say "own occupation", i.e., the inability to perform duties and tasks similar to your current job. You may prefer to purchase a policy that defines disability as the "own occupation." Why is that? You don't want to be a well-paid chef who relies on sight and smell to perform your job and be denied benefits because you are able to perform some less skilled, lower paid work. That won't help you meet your bills and maintain your lifestyle.

As with life insurance, search for companies that are highly rated and offer policies that are noncancelable.

### Health Insurance

Medical expenses arising from an accident or disease can add up quickly. While young adults do not typically face the more expensive medical issues of an older generation such as cancer, they are not immune to them either. If you are not covered by an employer health plan, it is wise to think about personal health insurance designed to protect you against outsized medical care costs such as hospitalization. Through the Affordable Care Act, health insurance policies are available to any individual who does not have access to an employer-provided plan.

You are in charge of your financial future. Smart choices will lead to good outcomes, and sacrifices today will reap rewards tomorrow. Great things are built on a foundation of hard work and supported by the accumulation of good decisions over time. And, like all long journeys, they begin with the modest start of a first step.

**Journal:**

How do you feel about your financial situation today? Does it fill you with fear, or are you feeling secure?

_____

_____

_____

What part of your game plan for life do you need to work on?

_____

_____

_____

_____

Does money dictate your happiness? If I ask someone else about you, would they give me the same answer?

_____

_____

_____

_____

What are you willing to shift in your thinking that will assist you in creating financial security?

_____

_____

_____

_____

Who are you accountable to to make sure these things happen? Who is going to help you design your plan for safety and success?

_____

_____

_____

_____

## Chapter Eleven:

## NOW WHAT?

This book is a call to action. It's time for you to process the ideas you've read and determine how you will shift your paradigm by turning the information into action. Reading about change is a start, but it is not enough. Taking steps to gain momentum is essential. Once you find your purpose, it will guide your appropriate sustainable actions.

Do you want to go back to school and finish your degree, or maybe get a master's degree? Perhaps you have been home with your children, and you need to get back into the work force. Maybe you have an invention, or a desire to start a new business, or an idea that you haven't moved on yet and you are not sure how to take action. The idea of getting started may be so overwhelming that it feels easier to just stay where you are.

Maybe you justify your indecision by saying, *I'm still praying about it.* I love prayer and believe that praying *is* taking action, but be careful of allowing prayer to replace action. The Father wants you to trust yourself as well; He sometimes waits for you to take the first step of faith and then He will meet you where you need Him most.

We are all human and posses certain limiting beliefs. Most of us have been burdened by the restrictive thoughts of other people— statements such as *you're too young to be successful,* or *you're too old to start a new career or hobby,* or *you're not the right color.* Whatever the limiting thought was, when it was planted in our minds, we had a choice in that moment as to how to respond. Unfortunately, when we first received many of these messages, we were too young or naïve or impressionable to understand that we had the choice to reject other people's ideas about us. We accepted them as truth, and they became our truth. Now is the time for you to redefine your truths. What limiting ideas have you been told? What was your response then, and what will it be now?

Your transition is your chance to start fresh. Of course, you will carry your past experiences forward with you, and while they will support your future, they don't need to define it. Living in the present and working toward your future with purpose is the key to freeing yourself from the internal prison of living in the past.

What does this mean? Well, it probably means that you have some work to do. Imagine that your life is a house. So far, you have built a nice, solid foundation with the skills and knowledge you have gathered and honed in your life up to this point. Every time you release yourself from someone else's limiting notions, you are filling in cracks in that foundation, making it even stronger.

Next, you will frame in the house, the place where you are going to live for the rest of your life, with *new* skills and knowledge. Every time you take a class, or learn a new skill, or work in a new job, or build a relationship with a new person, you are adding another room to your house.

Eventually, you will find yourself drawn to one room more than any other. You will bring more things—further knowledge, deeper experiences—into that room to make it more comfortable for you. You'll be creating a space where you are increasingly more productive, more confident, and more satisfied. And all the time, you'll have the knowledge that the other rooms you framed in are still full of potential. If the room you've moved into becomes restrictive, you can add on or remodel. Invite your trusted advisers—your new teammates—in to help you make decisions about which room to work on next. Ultimately, though, this is your house, and you decide what happens here.

So, go ahead, forget labels, forget the limiting expressions that other people have told you about yourself, and build your own

house. Step out of your comfort zone. Take that computer programming class, or that business administration class, or that job that's
going to make you push yourself.

But what if it turns out to be a waste of time? It may not be
the right thing for you, but *if you are open to learning lessons from
your mistakes*, it will not be a waste of time. You will gain something
from the experience, even if it's simply the knowledge that computer programming is not the room where you are going to spend
all your time.

I am very passionate about taking action. I see people dying all
around us, and some of you are still standing still, blaming others,
or waiting for someone else to do what you were designed to do.
Stop procrastinating, people!

In sports it is true that "fatigue makes a coward of us all." This
means that we haven't fulfilled our obligation to get in shape so
we can perform at a level of excellence. The same thing happens
in transition. We have to work out in our mental weight room; we
have to run the same mental success drills over and over until they
take the form of movement in the right direction. Are you ready to
step up?

It is time for you to stop allowing mediocre mind-set people
around you to hinder or even stifle your success. Separate from
them in some capacity, and get off the carousel of complacency.
I believe that habits linger in your mind, waiting to be picked up
again. These can either be good habits or bad habits. Which habits
are serving you now? When those bad habits come back around,
what will your response be? Your success follows your habits; if
your habits stink, so will you.

You have decisions to make. The past continues to whisper
in your ear and while those whispers can be encouraging, at times
they are discouraging because they remind us of where we've been,
and what choices we have made. It is time to take a stand while
deciding what and who will influence your actions moving forward
in your transition.

Listen and look for signs before and during your transition. They are all around you, and often when you least expect it, the impact is made. Early in my transition from the NFL, I was teaching a boot camp/athletic conditioning class at the Morrison YMCA in Charlotte, and this loud white dude was counting obnoxiously. I went to him and said "Dude, why are you counting so loudly?" He laughed, and we started up a conversation. He said to me, "You say the same things in your class that I say to my clients in my personal coaching practice." This random interaction assisted me in finding the career I'm thriving in today (Personal/Executive Coaching) and the guy, Rich Campe, has become one of my great friends.

What comes first? The action, result, or the thinking? As we mentioned earlier in the book, all action starts with a thought—the bible talks about how a small mustard seed reaps a greatest harvest. Our thoughts will reap whatever is being sown. I shared with my great friend Kenny going through transition, that it only takes one small step at a time to complete the journey. The objective is to keep moving forward. It's too easy to stop.

Hopefully this book has inspired and prepared you for the next chapter in your life. It is important to stay consistent in order to build different expectations within yourself while you are defining your destiny. Become a note taker, a reader, and a student in order to sustain true excellence. I have listed some books for you to read, and you'll find more on the website listed below.

You've got this: Believe it!  Take a deep breath and FOCUS on your direction.

As a free gift to you, we would like to offer every reader of this book a free online one-page **Life Transition 1.0 Assessment** that will help indentify your top potential strength and a potential weakness. This assessment is all about providing the necessary clarity for you to make better decisions during your transition. The assessment is based on proven, validated science that has been used over the past 80 years. Please take your free assessment by typing in www.beyondthelockerroombook.com/life. You can also learn more about our **Life Transition 2.0 Extended Assessment.**

Please go to www.beyondthelockerroombook.com and tell us briefly about a Beyond the Locker Room transition experience of your own. What happened in your journey that you could share to give hope to others or stop others from falling into a black hole of despair and confusion? What steps did you take to start building your new house?

In the service of others and continuing to transition ourselves, it is important that we plant seeds that will reap a harvest of success in the lives of others. I would love to read how this book has encouraged, motivated, or inspired you, so please feel free to email us at beyondthelockerroom@gmail.com or visit us online at www.beyondthelockerroombook.com.

# Resources

**Books:**

Bailey, Sebastian, PhD, and Octavius Black. *Mind Gym: Achieve More by Thinking Differently*. New York: HarperCollins, 2014.

Blanchard, Kenneth and Spencer Johnson. *The One Minute Manager*. New York: William Morrow and Company, 1981.

Bridges, William. *Managing Transitions: Making the Most of Change*. Cambridge: Da Capo Press, 2009.

Bridges, William. *Transitions: Making Sense of Life's Changes*. Cambridge: Da Capo Press, 2004.

Collins, Jim. *Good to Great: Why Some Companies Make the Leap... And Others Don't*. New York: HarperCollins, 2001.

Dweck, Carol S., PhD. *Mindset: The New Psychology of Success*. New York: Random House, 2008.

Johnson, Spencer. *Who Moved My Cheese?* New York: G. P. Putnam, 1998.

Patterson, Kerry, Joseph Grenny, Ron McMillan, and Al Switzler. *Crucial Conversations: Tools for Talking When Stakes are High*. New York: McGraw-Hill, 2002.

Sinek, Simon. *Start with Why: How Great Leaders Inspire Everyone to Take Action*. New York: Penguin, 2009.

Warren, Rick. *The Purpose Driven Life*. Grand Rapids, Mich.: Zondervan, 2002.

Wickman, Gino. Traction: *Get a Grip on Your Business*. Dallas: BenBella Books, 2012.


**Websites:**

www.my10minutecoach.com

www.nfl.com/legends

www.nflplayerengagement.com

www.playerstrust.com

## About The Author

Former NFL player turned dynamic speaker on the executive coaching circuit Leonard Wheeler has been a change agent for athletes, executives, and major corporations for fifteen years. His competitive spirit, power to motivate, and infectious personality have taken him all over the world. From serving on the boards of prominent national organizations to addressing corporations across the US and Europe and even the survivors of the Columbine tragedy, Leonard is highly sought after to motivate, train, coach, and lead.

As the President of Wheeler Enterprises, Inc., Leonard has worked with a variety of elite executives, athletes, and organizations, including NBA, Capital One, MIT, Vanguard, AAA, Carolinas Medical, MasterCard, Habitat for Humanity, the Tennessee Board of Education, AXA, Abbott, USO, and NFL, among many others. Leonard is the Central South Regional Director for the NFL, an Ambassador for the NFL, a selector for the NFL Sportsmanship Award, a member of the NFLPA Finance Committee, and a national speaker for the NFL's "Fuel Up To Play 60."

Leonard attended Troy University and played eight years in the NFL for the Cincinnati Bengals, the Minnesota Vikings, and the Carolina Panthers after being selected in the third round of the 1992 NFL Draft. He holds a degree in Business Administration and another in Communications, as well as certifications from Coachville, Change Essentials, Managing Millennials, and the Human Element. Learn more at www.leonardwheeler.com.

CPSIA information can be obtained
at www.ICGtesting.com
Printed in the USA
FSOW02n1618071117
40747FS